Teaching Practices from America's Best Urban Schools

Discover the teaching practices that make the biggest difference in student performance! The new edition of this practical, research-based book gives leaders and teachers an even closer look at instructional practices from top award-winning urban schools. With refreshed examples from high-performing teachers and detailed analyses of these practices, the authors demystify the achievement of these schools while offering a practical guide to help educators apply these practices in their contexts. *Teaching Practices from America's Best Urban Schools* is a valuable tool for any educator in both urban and non urban schools that serve diverse student populations, including English language learners and children from low-income families.

What's New

♦ Additional "What It Is/What It Isn't" boxes help educators distinguish the subtle differences in the implementation of practices that lead to impressive learning results.

♦ "Practice Guides" and "Practical Next Steps" for each of the 8 Success Factors encourage self-assessment and collaboration.

♦ Expansion of topics address current developments in education and additional examples from award-winning elementary, middle, and high schools provide new insights.

Joseph F. Johnson, Jr., Ph.D., is the Executive Director of the National Center for Urban School Transformation and Provost and Senior Vice President Emeritus, Dean Emeritus of the College of Education, and Professor Emeritus of Educational Leadership at San Diego State University, USA.

Cynthia L. Uline, Ph.D., is Professor Emeritus of Educational Leadership at San Diego State University, USA.

Lynne G. Perez, Ph.D., served as the Deputy Director of the National Center for Urban School Transformation at San Diego State University, USA.

Other *EYE ON EDUCATION*
Books Available from Routledge
www.routledge.com/eyeoneducation

Teaching Practices from America's Best Urban Schools

A Guide for School and Classroom Leaders

Second Edition

Joseph F. Johnson, Jr.,
Cynthia L. Uline, and
Lynne G. Perez

Routledge
Taylor & Francis Group

NEW YORK AND LONDON

Second edition published 2019
by Routledge
52 Vanderbilt Avenue, New York, NY 10017

and by Routledge
2 Park Square, Milton Park, Abingdon, Oxon, OX14 4RN

Routledge is an imprint of the Taylor & Francis Group, an informa business

First edition published by Eye on Education 2012

Library of Congress Cataloging-in-Publication Data
Names: Johnson, Joseph F., Jr., author.
Title: Teaching practices from America's best urban schools :
  a guide for school and classroom leaders / by Joseph F. Johnson, Jr.,
  Cynthia L. Uline, and Lynne G. Perez.
Description: Second Edition. | New York : Routledge, 2019. | "First edition
  published by Eye on Education 2012"—T.p. verso. | Includes
  bibliographical references.
Identifiers: LCCN 2019004793 | ISBN 9780815384441 (Hardback) |
  ISBN 9780815384458 (Paperback) | ISBN 9781351204354 (eBook)
Subjects: LCSH: Education, Urban—United States. | Students with social
  disabilities—United States. | Education—Parent participation—United States.
Classification: LCC LC5131 .J65 2019 | DDC 370.9173/2—dc23
LC record available at https://lccn.loc.gov/2019004793

ISBN: 978-0-8153-8444-1 (hbk)
ISBN: 978-0-8153-8445-8 (pbk)
ISBN: 978-1-351-20435-4 (ebk)

Typeset in Palatino
by Apex CoVantage, LLC

This book is dedicated
to our nation's greatest hope,
America's urban school teachers.

Contents

About the Authors

Joseph F. Johnson, Jr., Ph.D., is the Executive Director of the National Center for Urban School Transformation. He is also Provost and Senior Vice President Emeritus, Dean Emeritus of the College of Education, and Professor Emeritus within the Department of Educational Leadership at San Diego State University. He has previously served as a teacher, school, and district administrator, state education agency administrator in Texas and Ohio, researcher, technical assistance provider, and U.S. Department of Education official. His research focuses upon schools that achieve remarkable academic results for diverse populations of students. His work has appeared in journals such as *Education and Urban Society*, *Educational Administration Quarterly*, *Educational Leadership*, *International Journal of Leadership in Education*, *Journal of Education for Students Placed at Risk*, *Phi Delta Kappan*, and *Theory into Practice*. He is also an author of *Leadership in America's Best Urban Schools* and *Five Practices for Improving the Success of Latino Students: A Practical Guide for Secondary School Leaders*.

Cynthia L. Uline, Ph.D., is Professor Emeritus of Educational Leadership at San Diego State University. Cynthia's research explores the influence of built learning environments on students' learning, as well as the roles leaders, teachers, and the public play in shaping learning spaces. Her current research considers the potential of green schools as student-centered, ecologically responsive, and economically viable places for learning. She has published books and articles related to leadership for learning, leadership preparation, and the improvement of social and physical learning environments. Her work has appeared in journals such as *Educational Administration Quarterly*, *Teacher College Record*, *Journal of School Leadership*, *Journal of Education for Students Placed at Risk*, *International Journal of Leadership in Education*, *Journal of Research and Development in Education*, and *Educational Leadership*. Her recent book, entitled *Leadership for Green Schools: Sustainability for Our Children, Our Communities, and Our Planet*, co-authored with Lisa A.W. Kensler, was published by Routledge in 2017. She is also an author of *Leadership in America's Best Urban Schools*.

Lynne G. Perez, Ph.D., served as the Deputy Director of the National Center for Urban School Transformation at San Diego State University. She served as an executive coach in the center's Advancing Principal Leadership in Urban Schools Program. She also served as a lecturer with San Diego State's Department of Educational Leadership. Her work on school leadership issues has appeared in journals such as *Educational Administration Quarterly*, *Educational Leadership*, *Journal of Education for Students Placed at Risk*, *Journal of Educational Leadership*, *Journal of School Leadership*, and *Teacher College Record*. She is also an author of *Leadership in America's Best Urban Schools*.

Acknowledgments

This book exists because there are outstanding teachers, administrators, and support staff who have created outstanding learning environments for diverse groups of students in urban communities. We respect, acknowledge, and appreciate your impressive work. Also, we appreciate your willingness to open your schools to us and allow us to learn from your work. We hope this book is an affirmation of your impressive accomplishments, as well as a source of motivation as you continue to strive for excellence.

We also acknowledge and appreciate the many individuals—including school administrators, graduate students, professors, and teachers—who have engaged with us in visiting and studying America's high-performing urban schools. Your time, energy, and insights have been priceless as we have sought to better understand teaching and learning in outstanding urban schools.

We must also acknowledge that the study of high-performing urban schools is not new. Our work builds upon a tradition of scholarship and inquiry started by heroic educators such as Ron Edmonds, Larry Lezotte, and Wilbur Brookover and extended through the work of others such as Karin Chenoweth, Ron Ferguson, John Hattie, Kati Haycock, Ellen Moir, Anthony Muhammad, Pedro Noguera, Doug Reeves, James Scheurich, and Linda Skrla. These leaders constructed the foundation upon which this effort was built.

We especially acknowledge the strong support of San Diego State University. A former SDSU President, Stephen Weber, and a former Dean of SDSU's College of Education, Lionel "Skip" Meno, envisioned a national center that would identify, study, and promote excellence in urban schools. They secured initial funding support from the Qualcomm Corporation, and they creatively provided other support that helped us start the National Center for Urban School Transformation (NCUST). Subsequent university leaders have continued this strong support, even in difficult financial times.

San Diego State University has been a great home for NCUST, in part because of the outstanding faculty, staff, and students who have been important collaborators in our efforts. We have been enriched by opportunities to work with and learn from our colleagues in the Educational Leadership Department at San Diego State University, including Doug Fisher, Nancy Frey, Ian Pumpian, Cheryl James Ward, Vicki Park, and James Wright. Their efforts to study and promote equity-driven leadership have influenced our thinking about schools that generate outstanding learning results for all students.

As well, our partnership with colleagues in the Dual Language and English Learner Department at San Diego State has lead us to deeper understandings of equity and excellence in dual-language academies and schools that serve students with emerging bilingualism well. In particular, we appreciate the partnership of Cristina Alfaro, Sera Hernandez, Saul Maldonado, Margarita Machado-Casas, and Alberto Esquinca.

Finally, we acknowledge the time, wisdom, and commitment of our colleagues and staff at NCUST. We are honored to work with and learn from a team of executive coaches who have experience leading and/or supporting high-performing urban schools. NCUST was initiated and shaped through the work of former executive coaches, superintendents-in-residence, and leaders Barbra Balser, Tony Burks, Gina Gianzero, Karen Janney, Hazel Rojas, and Christina Theokas. Today, the Center flourishes through the work of current executive coaches and superintendents-in-residence Rupi Boyd, Debbie Costa-Hernandez, Shirley Peterson, Cara Riggs, and Granger Ward. These talented individuals have committed themselves to identifying, studying, and promoting the best practices of America's best urban schools. This book would not exist without their efforts.

Preface

Someone might ask, "Whatever happened to the American dream? Isn't this supposed to be the country where any child, regardless of race, ethnicity, language background, or family income, can aspire to academic, social, and economic success? Isn't this supposed to be the country where parents can expect that their children will grow up and enjoy a better standard of living than they experienced? What happened to the idea that every American child could access a quality education: a gateway to his or her dreams?"

Data suggest a different reality. High school graduation rates, standardized test scores, college completion rates, and almost any other indicator of academic accomplishment make the United States look more like a caste system than a nation of opportunity. One need consider only five variables—race/ethnicity, language background, family income, gender, and zip code—to accurately determine how the overwhelming majority of children will fare in our educational systems. What happened to the American dream?

The dream still lives in a few hundred remarkable schools across the nation. It has been our honor to identify, celebrate, and study amazing schools that achieve outstanding results for every demographic group they serve. This book is about schools that face impressive challenges associated with urban life—including poverty, crime, the lack of social services, and big-city bureaucracies—yet meet these challenges with impressive resolve, strong leadership, and effective teaching. Since 2006, the National Center for Urban School Transformation (NCUST) has been identifying, awarding, and studying many of the nation's highest-achieving urban schools. These schools provided multiple evidences of success (e.g., state assessment scores, graduation rates, attendance rates, discipline data, English-acquisition data, course-taking patterns) for their students in general. Additionally, the schools provided evidence that each racial/ethnic group served in these schools performed at levels above the average for all students throughout the state. As well, many of the schools demonstrated outstanding learning results for students with emerging bilingualism (Nieto, 2013, p. 75) and other groups of students who have traditionally been underserved by U.S. schools. Between 2006 and 2018, we visited, studied, and awarded 150 remarkable elementary, middle, and high schools that (1) served predominantly low-income students, (2) did not use selective admissions criteria, and (3) achieved outstanding results for every racial/ethnic group served. This book is based on what we learned from educators in these typical schools that achieved very atypical results.

Specifically, this book covers the nature of teaching in these schools. Through this book, we attempt to capture and describe the teaching practices that help set these high-performing schools apart from their counterparts.

We hope that the information presented here can inspire, inform, and reinforce efforts to improve teaching and learning in thousands of urban schools in the United States. At the same time, we know that many practices described here are effectively implemented in schools that serve diverse populations of students in suburban and rural areas.

Our studies of outstanding schools have helped us understand that educators, through their daily practice in classrooms, can rekindle the American dream. Through this book, we endeavor to pass the flame.

Intended Audience

This book is about teachers and written for teachers who are committed to generating excellent and equitable learning results for their students. We expect that this book will be useful to teachers and all those who support teachers, including principals, assistant principals, deans, superintendents, area superintendents, executive directors, principal supervisors, and many other school and district administrators. As well, we expect this book to be helpful to teacher leaders with many different job titles (such as lead teacher, department chair, resource teacher, helping teacher, team leader, resource specialist, teacher on specialist assignment, math specialist, reading specialist, science specialist, or technology specialist) and teacher leaders with no title at all. This volume is intended to be useful to any teacher (or future teacher) who is striving to influence the academic success of all students and all demographic groups of students.

Finally, we hope this book will be useful to individuals who, like us, are struggling to better understand why some teachers are able to lift their students to high levels of performance, while teachers in other schools with similar demographics and challenges work hard yet fail to make a sustainable difference on any measurable outcomes. We hope that our findings influence further study of schools that achieve excellent and equitable learning results so that, as a profession, we continuously improve our support of teachers who are committed to transforming their schools and districts so that all children achieve academic excellence, develop and sustain a love of learning, and graduate well prepared to succeed in post-secondary education, the workplace, and their communities.

About the Schools Studied, Awarded, and Featured in This Book

Each year since 2006, the NCUST publishes and disseminates a set of award criteria (see Appendix A); solicits nominations from state superintendents, local urban superintendents, and leaders of schools that won various national and state-level distinctions; and begins a rigorous process of identifying schools for the America's Best Urban Schools Award (previously called the National Excellence in Urban Education Award). For the sake of consistency, in this book, we refer to all of the awardees as recipients of the America's Best Urban School Award.

From the beginning, the award program was designed to identify schools that achieved both excellent and equitable learning results. We wanted to award schools that demonstrated a variety of learning results that exceeded state averages. We looked for urban schools with learning results (e.g., student success rates, graduation rates, state assessment scores, attendance rates, etc.) that were comparable to the results achieved in respected suburban schools. At the same time, we insisted that award winners demonstrate considerable evidence of high rates of academic success for all demographic groups they served, specifically students of color and students from families who met low-income criteria. Some of the schools awarded might be considered turnaround schools because they improved dramatically over a short period of time. Other award-winning schools had a long history of impressive academic successes.

Schools could not earn the America's Best Urban Schools Award simply by achieving strong overall learning results. Instead, schools were also required to provide evidence that every racial/ethnic/income group served was achieving at rates that exceeded state averages. We sought to identify, award, and study schools that evidenced both excellence and equity in learning results. This focus on both equity and excellence makes the America's Best Urban Schools Award different from many other award programs. For example, some programs focus solely on measures of excellence without attention to the levels of attainment of the diverse groups of students served. As well, some award programs focus solely on schools that demonstrate impressive progress for diverse populations of students. Also, some award programs (like the National Blue Ribbon Schools Program) include two separate and distinct programs, one focused on excellence (high rates of academic attainment) and one focused on equity (growth for diverse populations of students). In contrast, NCUST has sought to award and study urban schools with evidence of both excellence and equity in student learning outcomes. Additional information about the schools NCUST awarded and studied can be found in Appendix B.

Success Factors

Many factors contributed to the success of these urban schools; however, a central factor was the nature and quality of teaching. Teaching in these high-performing schools was qualitatively different from teaching in urban schools that achieved mediocre academic results. Through this book, we explain how teaching was different in these high-performing urban schools. We relate how teaching looked, sounded, and felt. We dissect excellent, effective instruction in ways that make it more understandable and replicable.

We have been inspired by the effectiveness of instruction in high-performing urban schools. Students learned more because they were taught in ways that made it easier for them to learn. Students learned more because teachers worked systematically to ensure each student's progress. In particular, diverse groups of students learned more because of the nature of the learning environments established by their teachers. Ultimately, all students learned more because teachers demanded nothing less of their students and of themselves.

During the past several years, many states have adopted more rigorous academic standards and more challenging state assessments. In most states, these new learning expectations demand the teaching of concepts and skills that are more advanced and complex than the standards previously adopted. In the schools featured in this book, we observed classrooms where students were demonstrating the academic knowledge and intellectual skills these new standards require. In the schools we studied, teaching practices promoted the depth of understanding and the applied use of knowledge that characterize many new state standards. To ensure all urban students learn challenging standards, the teaching practices described in this book are essential.

Through our examination of many pages of field notes, observation records, and interviews of teachers, principals, and students, we condensed our findings into eight practices, illustrated in Figure P. 1. As we shared our findings with educators from several of these high-performing schools, they affirmed that these are the essential practices they envisioned and pursued. As well, we have shared these findings with award-winning teachers, including Carlston Family Foundation award-winning teachers and various local and statewide teacher-of-the-year awardees who have described how they integrate these practices into their everyday teaching efforts. Each chapter of this book (Chapters 1 through 8) describes one of the eight practices in detail.

We saw examples of the practices described in this book consistently, but not universally, throughout these schools. We never heard anyone at any of these

Figure P.1

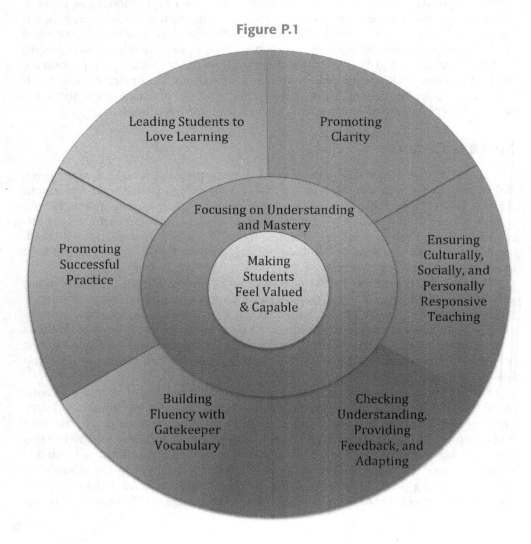

high-performing schools claim perfection. In fact, principals, teachers, support staff, parents, and students were often impressively open in describing the areas where they still had room to grow. Nonetheless, in these high-performing urban schools, we found a significant core of teachers who regularly exhibited many of the practices described in this book.

Conversely, in our work with struggling schools, we often find a small number of teachers modeling the teaching practices we discuss in this book. Unfortunately, in struggling schools, best teaching practices seem to be best kept secrets because there is little effort to learn about and emulate these practices throughout the school.

It is important to note that we saw the same core practices in successful elementary, middle, and high schools. Certainly, high school math classes looked different from middle school social studies classes and even more different from primary-grade reading classes; however, the same core teaching practices were evident in classrooms across age groupings. The similarities in instructional practices were far more striking than the differences.

Cautions

Schools change. Just as we have been thrilled to see urban schools achieve dramatic improvements in learning results over four or five years, we have been stunned to see precipitous declines in performance over a similar amount of time. Success comes from practices that are implemented each day and systems that promote the refinement of those practices over time. When educators stop implementing the practices that promote great learning results and when systems fail to promote continuous improvement, growth diminishes and stops. Sometimes, the schools we once celebrated fade into mediocrity.

Leadership matters. We have seen both positive and negative swings in learning results accompany changes in school leadership. In particular, principal leadership can have a substantial influence. On the other hand, some of the impressive schools we have studied have continued to improve and excel, even after principal turnover. In some cases, new leaders are able to reinforce and strengthen the systems that promoted outstanding teaching practices. In other cases, new leaders fail to understand and sustain what educators need in order to keep improving outcomes for students.

We would love to be able to guarantee that the schools described in this book continue to achieve excellent and equitable learning results for their students, but we can't. However, we can guarantee that student learning will improve when schools implement systems that promote, refine, and sustain the practices that influenced impressive successes in the schools we have awarded and studied.

Contents of the Book

As illustrated in Figure 0.1, at the heart of effective teaching efforts in high-performing schools, we saw practices that resulted in students feeling valued, capable, and loved. We discuss the centrality of these practices in Chapter 1. In particular, teachers interacted in ways that led all students (regardless of race, ethnicity, language background, or family income) to believe that teachers cared enough to help ensure their academic success and their success in life.

Chapter 2 describes the focus on understanding and mastery that typified instruction in these schools. Teachers focused persistently and doggedly on leading all children to understand and master key academic concepts and skills. While many urban schools sabotage their improvement efforts by rigidly trying to "cover" all of the standards or by insisting that teachers "keep pace" with a pacing guide, these more successful schools chose to focus on getting their students to learn key academic content. Again, as illustrated in Figure P. 1, these first two practices highlight the overarching sense of purpose that influences how the other six practices are pursued.

Chapters 3 through 8 describe pedagogical techniques that influenced the extent to which students felt valued and capable, as well as the extent to which students understood challenging academic content. Chapter 3 describes the manner in which teachers developed clarity about what they wanted students to learn, while Chapter 4 specifically focuses on the manner in which teachers designed lessons that responded to the cultural, social, and personal backgrounds, interests, and strengths of their students. Chapter 5 describes how teachers checked for student understanding, provided feedback, and adapted instruction accordingly. Chapter 6 explains how teachers endeavored to ensure that students developed fluency with the essential vocabulary associated with the lesson, and Chapter 7 explains how teachers promoted successful independent practice and minimized the time students spent "practicing" incorrectly. Chapter 8 explains how teachers inspired students to learn more.

In Chapter 9, the final chapter, we describe factors that influence schoolwide change in the improvement of the eight teaching practices. In particular, we offer concrete suggestions as teacher leaders and school administrators address the challenge of improving longstanding teaching practices throughout their schools. We note that in high-performing urban schools, we find coherent educational improvement systems that enhance the likelihood of improved teaching and learning for all groups of students. This final chapter offers suggestions that can support teams of educators as they endeavor to make a positive difference in the lives of their students.

What's New in This Edition

While the eight teaching practices described in the first edition are fundamentally the same, we have refined the language we use to discuss several of the practices in ways that hopefully provide a more accurate, clear picture of the teaching practices we found in the schools we studied. Also, this edition includes many more examples of the outstanding teaching practices we observed. In particular, we included many examples from schools we studied and awarded since the first edition was published.

The organization of each chapter in this edition is similar to the organization of chapters in the first edition. Each chapter (1 through 8) provides examples from lessons observed in actual classrooms within high-performing elementary, middle, and high schools. Each chapter begins with a vignette from an actual classroom, followed by a detailed discussion of the practice. We try to explain in detail with rich examples. A new feature is a "perpetual question" that frames the thinking of educators in high-performing urban schools.

Similar to the first edition, each chapter includes a section entitled *What It Is & What It Isn't*. Often educators assume they understand a practice and are implementing it well, when in fact their understanding is considerably different from how we have seen the practice implemented in high-performing urban schools. In this section of each chapter, we aim to distinguish the subtle differences in the implementation of the practice that lead to impressive learning results for all demographic groups of students.

Also, each chapter (from Chapter 1 through 8) includes a practice guide that might be used in multiple ways. Teachers can use these guides as self-assessments. Teachers might ask themselves, "In my lesson today, how many of these items did I accomplish?" Alternately, among a group of teachers endeavoring to maximize a practice, teachers might use one of the guides to observe each other and provide feedback. Similarly, in schools committed to increasing the successful implementation of a practice, administrators might use the guide as an organizing framework for professional development activities, as a tool for conducting classroom visits and observations, and/or as a vehicle for offering teachers feedback about the extent to which they are making progress in implementing the practice.

Each guide offers suggestions about evidence that might be indicative of the practice. As school teams consider the various guides, additional ideas may emerge as appropriate supplements or replacements. Each item is only a piece of evidence that may or may not reflect full implementation of the practice. Nonetheless, the guide may be helpful as educators seek to improve their implementation.

Some of the guides allow "yes" or "no" responses. Even in outstanding lessons, it is rare to find "yes" answers to all of the items in a guide. A lesson is probably strong if half of the items are identified affirmatively. Great lessons might evidence three-fourths or more of the items. Other guides offer more opportunities for short responses.

Finally, each chapter (1–8) includes a Practical Next Steps section. This new feature is intended to offer practical suggestions to educators who wish to build their proficiency with the teaching practice addressed in the chapter. While the Practical Next Steps can be used by anyone, they might be most useful to teams of educators who wish to support each other in advancing their practice so that all demographic groups of students are more likely to learn challenging academic content and skills.

How to Use This Book

We believe this book can have the greatest impact when teams of educators read, study, and use this book together. We hope that teachers, instructional coaches, department chairs, and school administrators come together to read and discuss the practices described in this book. Certainly, we believe that the practices described can be useful in urban elementary, middle, and high schools; however, we believe that the practices can help any school improve its effectiveness in ensuring that all children experience academic success. We hope that teams of educators come together and ask themselves, "How are our practices similar to and different from the practices described in this book?" In particular, we hope that educators will go into each other's classrooms so that they acquire objective information that helps them affirm their pedagogical strengths and identify opportunities for growth. While individuals can certainly use this book to hone their teaching practices, we have learned that teamwork is an essential ingredient in the success of outstanding schools. As well, we hope that this book is more than just a topic for the next random act of professional development. Instead, we hope that this book inspires a deep commitment to ongoing efforts to improve professional practice. As we note in Chapter 9, change requires focused, persistent effort. Change is more likely to be achieved when a coherent system of structures affords teachers many opportunities to try new approaches, receive constructive feedback, reflect, refine, and try again.

Reference

Nieto, S. (2013). *Finding joy in teaching students of diverse backgrounds: Culturally responsive and socially just practices in U.S. classrooms*. Portsmouth, NM: Heinemann.

1 Making Students Feel Valued and Capable

A group of six high school students from Dayton Business and Technology High School met with a researcher from the National Center for Urban School Transformation (NCUST). The researcher asked, "How did you happen to attend this school?"

One male student quickly responded, "Most of us were kicked out of other schools."

Another male affirmed, "Yeah. We got expelled because of stuff."

"So, how long will you attend this school?" the researcher asked.

"Oh, I'm not going back to my other school," one girl quickly explained.

"Me either!" other students offered in chorus.

"Almost all of us plan on graduating from this school," one of the girls explained.

"Is that because you're not allowed to return to your previous schools?" the researcher asked.

"No," one of the boys responded, while adding, "We could go back after one month, one semester, or one year, depending on what we did. But, we don't want to go back. We want to graduate from this school."

Before the researcher could ask why, one of the girls explained, "The teachers at this school care about us. They want us to learn."

Another chimed in, "Yeah, they want us to graduate. They believe in us."

"But, don't all teachers care?" inquired the researcher.

"Not at my other school. At least, they didn't care about me," responded one of the boys.

"At this school, the teachers really want you to understand things," one girl added.

"What do you mean?" inquired the researcher.

The girl responded, "At the other schools, the teachers just want to get done with whatever they're supposed to do, give you an assignment, and give you a 'D' or 'F' grade. They don't really care if you learn it or not. They just want a grade for their gradebook."

"Yeah, but here it's different," another student explained. "They're always trying to break it down for us so we understand it."

"What do you mean?" the researcher asked.

The girl explained, "Like, they're always trying to make it real for us. The teachers are always trying to make things make sense to us. They really want us to understand."

After a brief pause, the researcher asked, "So, do you feel you work harder here than you worked at your previous schools?"

In unison, the students nodded affirmatively. Then, the researcher asked, "Why do you work harder at this school?"

One of the boys answered, "Why do we work so hard? Well, you know that most of us kids went to other schools around here, and we were kicked out or suspended or other stuff happened." Then gesturing with his arms crossed, as if imitating his former teachers, he continued, "At my other school the teachers would see me coming and think 'Here comes trouble. Here comes a headache. Here comes my next suspension. Here comes a dropout.' They saw me as another Black statistic. Even though I knew I wasn't stupid, I pretty much figured they were right. I was never good at school. I had a hard time reading the textbooks. I just didn't see how I was going to get anywhere at school or in life."

He continued to explain, "So, when I came here, I thought it would be all about hanging with my friends. But, when I got here, the teachers saw me differently." Then gesturing with his arms wide open, he continued, "They looked at me like 'Here comes potential. Here comes a future graduate. Here comes a future college student.' That's the way they treated me. That's the way they talk to all of us. So, when you're treated that way, it just makes everything different. You want to work hard because you want them [the adults] to be right about you. You don't want them to change their minds."

Dayton Business and Technology High School is a charter school in Dayton, Ohio. The school won the America's Best Urban School Award in 2013.

A Perpetual Question

On the Minds of Educators Striving to Produce Equity and Excellence

How can I get each and every one of my students to believe, "My teacher sincerely wants me to succeed in life and my teacher is confident that I can succeed"?

In schools where diverse groups of students excel, teachers lead all students to feel valued and capable. In the first edition of this book, we discussed this phenomenon as one of eight key teaching practices. However, after visiting and studying many more outstanding urban schools, we acknowledge the centrality of making students feel valued and capable to the other seven practices. Thus, Figure 1.1 illustrates that the practice of making students feel valued and capable is at the heart of the effective instructional practices we found in the high-performing urban schools we studied. Efforts to implement the other seven practices are less likely to influence learning results if they are not implemented in a manner that results in students feeling valued and capable.

Scheurich (1998) studied schools that generated strong academic results for children of color and children from low-income families. He determined that educators in those schools established caring, loving, and respectful environments in which students were expected to achieve at high levels. Similarly, in every high-performing school we studied, students (including students at the Dayton Business Technology High School referenced above) emphasized that their teachers cared sincerely about them and their academic success. We believe that almost all teachers care about their students; however, students in high-performing urban schools are much more likely to *perceive* that their teachers care about them and value them. The perception of caring, or lack thereof, influences student motivation and behavior.

Noddings (2005) emphasized that care and students' perception of care were likely to influence student success. Ferguson (2002) specifically noted that Black and

Figure 1.1

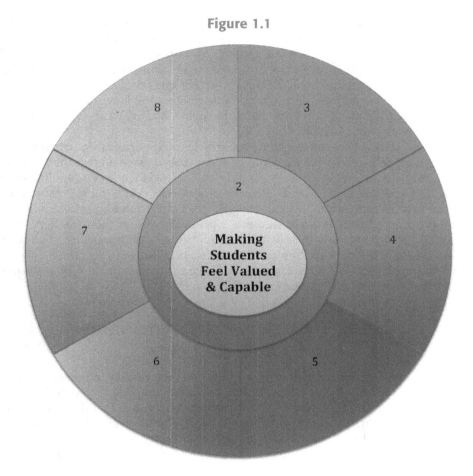

Latino students' perceptions of their teachers' caring influenced their level of effort even more than did White students' perceptions of their teachers' caring.

After visiting 150 high-performing urban schools where all demographic groups of students excelled, we are convinced that teachers in these schools lead students to feel valued, respected, and capable. In more typical schools, the same students are often left to feel alienated, unwanted, and unlikely to succeed. Teachers in high-performing urban schools convince Black, Latino, and Native American students, students from low-income or immigrant families, students with emerging bilingualism, LGBTQ students, students experiencing homelessness, students in foster care, students with disabilities, and many other students that the adults in the school value and respect them. Somehow, students (including students who are commonly not served well in urban communities) become convinced that their teachers are committed to helping them succeed in school and in life.

Throughout this chapter, we use the term "caring" extensively. We note, however, that Noddings (1984) and Valenzuela (1999) described "aesthetic caring" that occurs in ineffective schools where educators demonstrate "care" when students conform to educators' expectations. The veneer of aesthetic caring wears thin quickly in environments where students are accustomed to the frustrations and disappointments associated with poverty, violence, and racism. In contrast, Noddings and Valenzuela explained that, through authentic caring, educators nurture and value relationships with all students. In this second edition, we have endeavored to distinguish the authentic caring we observed in the high-performing schools we studied. We have attempted to explain what authentic caring looks like and why this type of caring is difficult to develop and sustain.

It is important to emphasize that students in high-performing urban schools perceived that their teachers cared about them *and* they perceived that their teachers believed they were capable of succeeding. In contrast, Fisher, Frey, Quaglia, Smith, and Lande (2018) reported that 27 percent of students don't think their teachers expect them to be successful. This percentage is likely higher among students served in typical urban schools. Among students who perceive that their teachers doubt their ability to succeed, only the most resilient or those with the strongest supports at home are likely to thrive academically. Thus, a central factor in the success of high-performing urban schools is their ability to create environments in which students perceive that they are both valued and capable.

Caring Enough to Know and Value Individual Students

Hattie (2009) synthesized over 800 studies of factors that influenced student achievement. He found that teacher–student relationships have a major influence on student learning, more powerful than most pedagogical practices. While this finding might not surprise many, Klem and Connell (2004) found a lack of urgency on the part of many educators to establish and nurture strong positive relationships with students, even in the face of growing evidence that such relationships influence student academic performance.

In our interviews and focus groups with hundreds of students from high-performing urban schools, students used the adjective "caring" to describe their teachers more than any other descriptor. Students used the metaphor of family more than any other to describe their school. "It's like a family here. People care about you," students explained.

A factor that influences positive teacher–student relationships is the extent to which teachers succeed in getting to know and understand the students they teach. Often, in urban schools, teachers come from different racial/ethnic, socio-economic, and linguistic backgrounds than the students they serve. Perhaps, in our typical pre-service and in-service teacher preparation programs, we underestimate the chasms created by these differences. Too often, educators graduate from teacher preparation programs assuming they will teach students who share their backgrounds, interests, curiosities, and motivations. Conversely, too often, educators graduate from teacher preparation programs with assumptions that urban students have dramatically different backgrounds, interests, curiosities, and motivations. Neither set of assumptions is an appropriate substitute for the time and energy necessary to get to know students and their families. The greater the social distance between educators and students, the more essential it is for educators to spend time getting to know who they have the privilege to serve.

Fisher et al. (2018) reported that only 52 percent of students believe their teachers know their name. Additionally, only 67 percent of students indicated that they feel accepted at school for who they are. The lack of personal connection and acceptance create major learning barriers for many students. In contrast, students at high-performing urban schools reported that their teachers cared enough to get to know them, to build relationships, and to establish bonds.

For example, at O'Farrell Charter School in San Diego, California, each teacher is assigned a group of students with whom he or she meets daily. Teachers get to know their "homebase" students, their social/emotional needs and strengths, and their families. Similarly, teachers at MacArthur High School in Houston, Texas, explained how school administrators took them on tours of the surrounding neighborhood so that teachers could learn more about their students, their families, and the real challenges students faced. Beyond the neighborhood tours, MacArthur administrators expected teachers to make regular phone calls to parents. While these calls might have been difficult for some teachers initially, teachers reported that they came to appreciate how many of the parents were eager to see their child succeed in school (Gonzalez, 2015).

At International Elementary in Long Beach, California, one of the teachers established a mentor program. Almost every staff person at the school serves as a mentor to a student. Teachers meet with their mentees weekly and talk about whatever the student wants to discuss. These and similar efforts help ensure that students feel valued.

When Rose Longoria was assigned to serve as principal of Pace High School in Brownsville, Texas, her first priority was to help her faculty build relationships with their students. She wanted to help teachers spend time getting to know the students. She asserted, "We need to understand our students. We need to build relationships. Let's find out why they are struggling." By encouraging teachers to dig deeper to understand the reasons behind student issues, the principal urged teachers beyond aesthetic caring and helped teachers learn more about the strengths, needs, hopes, and fears of students and their families. These efforts to better know and understand the students helped develop stronger relationships between teachers and students.

For example, toward the end of the class period, a Pace teacher enthusiastically asked her students, "How many of you will be at my tutorial session immediately after school?" Many students raised their hands, and the teacher cheered while emphasizing what the students would learn during the after-school session. However, the teacher noticed one boy who did not raise his hand. As the period ended and students began to leave, the teacher approached the student who did not raise his hand, smiled, and said, "I'm hoping I will see you at the tutorial session this afternoon."

The student responded, "No, I can't because I have to work."

The teacher continued the conversation, saying, "You have been making such great progress and you are so close to mastering this topic. I know if you could attend the tutorial, it would really help you."

"But, I can't cause I have to work," the student said quietly.

The teacher paused for a moment and then offered, "How about if you come in early tomorrow morning and I'll provide a special tutorial session for you?"

The student looked up at the teacher and quickly said, "I'll be here. What time?"

The teacher took a little extra time to get to understand the student's situation. She understood that the student's job was an important source of income for his family. She also recognized that the student had the potential to break out of the cycle of poverty and excel with the right support.

While race, ethnicity, language background, and socio-economic variables often create important barriers that have to be bridged, other relationship barriers are created by the trauma and stress students experience throughout their lives. Duncan-Andrade (2009) described the chronic stresses experienced by some students as a result of violence and loss. Teachers who are oblivious to the pains and frustrations students regularly endure might misinterpret students' anger as a personal affront or might misunderstand students' lack of affect as apathy or a lack of appreciation for the feelings of others, when in fact, the students' behavior may be a direct consequence of chronic stress.

For example, a teacher at Cecil Parker Elementary in Mount Vernon, New York, shared about a student who was not coming to school. One of the adults from the school visited the child's home and found him alone. After a lengthy discussion, the adult learned that the student was intentionally missing the school bus, because the bus route passed the street corner where his mother worked as a prostitute. The boy was petrified that his friends would recognize his mother on the street corner. In response, the school principal worked with the district transportation director to modify the bus route so that the bus avoided the intersection where the boy's mother worked. After the route change was made, the student had perfect attendance for the remainder of the year.

In high-performing urban schools, as teachers got to know students, they deliberately helped students feel valued and appreciated. Teachers established and maintained a rapport that helped students perceive teachers as approachable. Teachers demonstrated a genuine interest in their students' ideas, concerns, and aspirations. "My teachers here know my name and greet me whenever they see me," a sophomore at MacArthur High School in Houston, Texas, explained. "They make me feel like I'm somebody." Similarly, a student at Cecil Parker Elementary explained, "When I see my teacher in the hallway or after school, she asks me how my family is doing. She cares about me and she cares about all of us."

Throughout many interviews, students described how they perceived teachers cared about them personally. For example, a student at Lawndale High School in Los Angeles remarked:

> The teachers here are great. You feel like they're always there for you. You know they're more than just a teacher. They try to get close to you. If you don't understand something, if they see that you're down or there's something wrong, they come up to you and ask, "What's wrong?" And it's not only a teacher relationship but also someone you can trust.

When parents were interviewed, many emphasized the power of the personal relationships teachers maintained with students. "My daughter would do anything for that teacher," a Golden Empire Elementary (Sacramento, California) parent emphasized. "She [the teacher] has built a bond with my child in just a few months. But, that's like all the teachers here. They just care."

Similarly, a parent at Charles Lunsford Elementary in Rochester, New York, confessed, "Please don't tell anybody, but we moved to a different neighborhood, and we're not even supposed to be at this school anymore. But, when I tried to suggest to my kids that they would go to a different school, they all had a fit. So I drive across town every day. But it's worth it. These teachers know my kids. They know what makes them tick."

Caring Enough to Model Courtesy and Respect

Teaching styles may vary; however, teachers in high-performing schools demonstrated courtesy and respect in all interactions. As a student at Dandy Middle School in Fort Lauderdale declared, "They [teachers] give us respect, even when we don't deserve it."

Students (like all individuals) learn to interpret certain actions as demonstrations of courtesy, acknowledgement, or respect. Some actions may be broadly interpreted as disrespectful (e.g., name calling), while other more subtle nuances (e.g., forms of address, methods of correction, eye contact) may signal respect or disrespect within cultural groups. In high-performing urban schools, teachers know their students well enough to know what students interpret as courteous and respectful behavior, and they model such behavior with great consistency.

Students offered a variety of examples to illustrate the ways in which teachers treated them with respect. A junior at Lawndale explained, "If you mess up behavior-wise, they [teachers] don't get weird about it. They stay cool and calm, like they understand you may be going through a rough time. They don't make it worse than it is." A fifth-grade student at Benjamin Franklin Elementary in Bakersfield, California, explained, "If you get something wrong, they tell you that you're wrong, but they don't embarrass you in front of everybody." A fourth-grade student at Golden Empire Elementary in Sacramento, California, commented similarly, "If you don't finish your assignment, the teachers don't yell. They just make you stay in and finish the work."

It is important to note that students reported that their teachers were remarkably consistent in demonstrating courtesy and respect. "At my old school, I had teachers who would act like they cared about you sometimes, then when you did something wrong, they would go off," a Tucker Elementary student explained. "The teachers here are different. They show you respect no matter what you do. It makes you feel like you're special."

Caring Enough to Praise and Acknowledge

In both subtle and overt ways, effective teachers provide specific, meaningful praise in response to student effort. Because praise is frequent, students (even older students) have become accustomed to receiving praise from their teachers and from each other.

At high-performing urban schools, frequent verbal and written responses from students provide teachers many opportunities to acknowledge and praise student efforts. Positive acknowledgement of behavior, effort, and accomplishment was far more abundant in high-performing urban schools than in typical urban schools.

While in more typical schools, one might count one or two examples of teachers praising students in a short ten- or fifteen-minute observation, in high-performing schools it was common to observe several such examples in observations of similar length.

Perhaps most importantly, students perceived that the praise offered by their teachers was sincere. Often the perception of sincerity was supported by specificity. For example, a third-grade teacher at Horace Mann Elementary in Glendale, California, explained to a student, "I like the way you made a logical inference about the character." Similarly, a Hambrick Middle School (Houston, Texas) math teacher commented, "Nice explanation of the meaning of slope [in a linear equation]."

At Eastwood Middle School in El Paso, Texas, a teacher was overheard telling a group of students:

> I really appreciate the way you are thinking hard about this problem. It's a tough problem, but I believe you're going to solve it because you are thinking through the problem in a logical way.

In response, one of the students suggested to the group, "Let's see if we can diagram this problem a little differently. We must be getting close." Then another student added, "Yeah, we can solve this if we keep working together on it." In hundreds of examples like this, we observed students acting as if their teachers' praise was a personal validation from a knowledgeable, sincere, and reliable source. Students perceived that their teachers believed in their capacity to succeed, and students were eager to prove their teachers right.

In many high-performing elementary, middle, and high schools, praise took physical form on the walls of many classrooms and hallways. We observed far more attractively displayed examples of recent, high-quality student work in high-performing schools compared to what we found in more typical urban schools. Even in secondary schools, teachers posted outstanding examples of student work.

The posted work represented student efforts across multiple disciplines. In many schools, student writing was featured prominently. Typically, the posted work included positive teacher comments and grades. Often, the work was posted along with the academic objective the assignment was designed to measure. In many cases, teachers also posted a rubric or scoring guide that explained the criteria used to evaluate the assignment.

In some cases, students were eager to show the researchers their work on their classroom walls. "Hey mister, see this? I did this," a student at Bonham Elementary (Dallas, Texas) bragged. Students saw their work on school walls as an indication that they belonged and that they were successful.

Caring Enough to Demand the Best

Students in high-performing urban schools believed their teachers cared, in part because students perceived that their teachers taught challenging academic content, insisted upon good behavior, and demanded high-quality work. Irvine and Fraser (1998) described educators who cared in this manner as "warm demanders." Bondy and Ross (2008) explained that warm demanders knew their students as individuals, demonstrated unconditional positive regard, and then insisted that students perform to high standards. Ladson-Billings (2002) emphasized that caring educators demanded that students work hard to succeed. Johnson, Uline, and Perez (2017, p. 21) explained, "Warm demanders dominated the cultures of these high-performing urban schools." In particular, teachers served as warm demanders for every racial/ethnic/income group served.

Elementary, middle, and high school students from all racial and ethnic groups offered many examples of their teachers' high expectations as evidence of caring. For instance, at Franklin Towne Charter in Philadelphia, Pennsylvania, both White and Black students expressed pride in the rigor of the curriculum they were expected to master. "They [teachers] care because they could just give you easy work," one student explained, "but instead they push you to learn tough topics in math, science, and other subjects. When you leave this school, you're ready for college."

At KIPP Adelante in San Diego, California, a Latino middle school student expressed a similar sentiment by stating, "The teachers here want you to have a future. We're going to be able to get into the very best high schools. Our teachers make sure we're learning everything we need to learn." This student and others at KIPP Adelante accepted their teachers' high academic expectations as expressions of caring.

Often, teachers spent time explaining details about learning expectations and helping students understand how lessons were preparing them for later success in college, the workplace, or in other aspects of life. For example, at Maplewood Richmond Heights High School in St. Louis, Missouri, teachers posted model assignments associated with each lesson. Teachers explained to students the rigor associated with the model assignments, emphasizing how performance at the level of the model would be comparable to college-level expectations.

An educator at Westcliff Elementary in the Fort Worth Independent School District claimed, "Students don't feel loved if they're not held accountable." In high-performing urban schools, teachers insisted that students develop and demonstrate the ability to discuss the concepts they were learning and relate the concepts to real situations. In the high-performing urban schools, teachers demanded student accountability for demonstrating deep understanding of concepts and ideas. Teachers expected students to be able to explain, discuss, demonstrate, compare, apply, and utilize information. Even when state standards, teacher's guides, or textbooks demanded less, teachers pushed their students toward higher levels of thinking.

Frequently, educators conveyed caring and commitment as they insisted upon scholarly behavior. At Jim Thorpe Fundamental Academy in Santa Ana, California, teachers prepared students to behave as scholars. Signs on walls reminded students how to behave in a scholarly manner, and teachers referred to students as scholars. At Bursch Elementary in Compton, California, Black and Latino students knew they were being prepared to attend college. Their cooperative work groups were named for various colleges and universities. Students were eager to live up to their teachers' high expectations.

Students also indicated that their teachers' high expectations for their character and behavior were evidence of caring. "The teachers make sure that everybody follows the rules," an Escontrias Elementary (El Paso, Texas) Latino student explained. "There's almost never fights here. This is the safest school I've ever been to. The teachers make sure everybody is safe." At Franklin Towne Charter High School in Philadelphia, Pennsylvania, students expressed the same opinions. "I'm never scared in this building," a Black female sophomore stated. A White male senior reported, "I've been here since my freshman year. I've never seen a fight at school." Students emphasized that teachers, administrators, and support personnel worked hard to make sure they were safe. "You don't have to worry about being picked on or bullied at this school," a Black student at Cecil Parker Elementary in Mount Vernon, New York, explained. "Teachers make sure that you can do your work and be safe." Students in many of the high-performing schools echoed the belief that their teachers cared enough to create learning environments in which they and all other students were expected to adhere to strong codes of conduct.

Teachers reinforced expectations for positive student behavior by fairly and consistently enforcing reasonable rules. Students were expected to work hard, stay engaged in learning activities, and interact with each other in polite and respectful ways. When students did not follow rules, teachers responded calmly yet firmly. For example, a teacher at KIPP Adelante quietly and discretely gave her cell phone to a misbehaving student. The student gasped, took the phone, and quietly stepped outside the classroom door. He called his parent, discussed his behavior, and brought the phone back to his teacher. The routine was simple yet powerfully effective. The teacher did not raise her voice or show any emotion. The teacher did not waste any time with reminders, pleas, or threats.

Consistently, throughout high-performing urban schools, we observed similar firm, fair, and calm enforcement of rules and consequences. A student receiving special education services at Tucker Elementary in Long Beach, California, confessed, "Before I came to this school, I used to be in trouble all the time." When asked why things had changed, he explained, "The teachers here care about me. They want me to succeed in school. They like me, but they don't let me get away with anything. This is a good place to be."

Caring Enough to Transform Classroom Practices

The students at Dayton Business and Technology High School believed their teachers cared enough to transform how they taught so students were more likely to learn. Students perceived that the expectations their teachers maintained reflected a high level of caring. At the same time, students believed that their teachers cared enough to change classroom practices so students would have a high likelihood of meeting high expectations. For example, at Dayton Business and Technology High School, every teacher had committed to including a practical experiential component into every lesson they taught. Thus, on numerous occasions, students remarked, "Teachers at this school care. They make the learning real for us." At many of the high-performing urban schools studied, students offered detailed descriptions of the efforts their teachers made to provide them with relevant, authentic, motivating, and supportive learning experiences.

In more typical urban schools, many students fail because they find it difficult or impossible to succeed within the confines of the rules, routines, and teaching styles of their teachers. For example, some teachers might explain concepts using examples from textbooks to which students cannot relate. Other teachers might describe concepts using language, vocabulary, dialects, and/or syntax that students have difficulty understanding. Some might insist that students sit quietly and listen for long periods of time when the stresses of the previous night or the emptiness in their stomachs might make listening quietly require a herculean effort. In high-performing urban schools, we found that many students excelled, in large part because teachers were willing to transform classroom practices in ways that responded to student needs. We found *positive transformational cultures* in which teachers were constantly exploring ways to change teaching practices, processes, and routines so student success was more likely.

At Lawndale High School near Los Angeles, California, students described how the school's "No D" policy meant they had to work hard. They could not earn credit for courses by barely meeting the requirements for a D grade. They could earn an A, B, C, or a failing grade of F. Students acknowledged that the policy made them work hard; however, they also emphasized that part of the reason they worked so hard was that teachers worked hard to help them succeed. As one Lawndale student stated:

> We have great teachers who are always offering tutoring in the mornings and after school or during lunch. They're always there helping us and it's a challenge, but we always get the help we need. It just makes it a great place to be.

Students reported that extra support came from teachers in a variety of ways, including access to additional learning resources (especially technology resources and manipulatives), the presentation of varied examples (especially examples that make it easier for students to relate to concepts), and the availability of additional time. "Sometimes, it's hard for me to understand the science, so my teacher gives me extra time and extra help to make sure my notes make sense," a seventh-grade student at Horace Mann Dual Language Academy in Wichita, Kansas, explained. Similarly, a fourth-grade student at Dreamkeepers Academy in Norfolk, Virginia, reported, "My teacher finds ways to make hard stuff easier. Like, she found a CD that made it a lot easier to learn our math." Ultimately, we found that students perceived that their teachers cared enough to transform classroom practices in ways that were more likely to help them learn and succeed. A primary-grade student at Highland Elementary in Silver Spring, Maryland, emphasized, "If you think that you can't do something during class (like you think it's too hard for you), the teachers help you because they know that you can do the work."

It is important to note that teachers at high-performing urban schools do not lower their expectations. They demand effort. We rarely saw evidence that teachers diminished *what* they expected their students to learn; however, we saw many examples of teachers exploring *how* they would help students meet their learning expectations, even though students might have entered the class without the background knowledge, experiences, or resources that typically benefit other students. Teachers planned and delivered lessons that provided a quantity and quality of support that ensured students would succeed at learning challenging academic concepts, when they exerted reasonable effort. As a result, students felt capable and were willing to risk trying.

Caring Enough to Create Attractive and Educationally Rich Physical Environments

Educators in high-performing urban schools made a variety of efforts to use the physical environment to communicate positive regard for students. In particular, classrooms and learning environments were clean, attractive, well maintained, and conducive to learning. Students were proud of the places where they learned. In many high-performing urban schools, teachers posted high-quality student work to create a physical environment that celebrated student accomplishments.

"Look at this school. This doesn't look like a ghetto school," a fifth-grade student at Dreamkeepers Academy insisted. He pointed with pride to the attractive posters, the engaging displays, and the clean floors. Through posters, pictures, and other displays, the physical environment gives students tangible evidence that teachers have high expectations for their immediate and long-term academic success.

A growing body of research connects the quality of school facilities to student outcomes, including achievement, behavior, and attitudes about school. Uline, Tschannen-Moran, and Wolsey (2009) examined the link between school building quality and student outcomes through the mediating influence of school climate. From the data, several broad themes related to the quality of the learning environment emerged as central to this interaction between school facilities and learning, including movement, aesthetics, play of light, flexible and responsive classrooms, elbow room, and security. The physical environments of classrooms and other school facilities communicate powerful messages to students about the extent to which educators value them and believe they are capable of excelling.

Often when we take educators to visit high-performing urban schools, the visitors comment, "The campus was so clean," or "We didn't see any graffiti," or "How do they manage to have such attractive classrooms and hallways?" Visitors are not the only ones who notice. We have heard parents say, "This is the nicest building in our neighborhood and I'm proud to send my child here." As well, we have heard students comment, "Any kid would be proud to go to school here."

Several administrators in high-performing urban schools explained to us that their buildings were not immune to vandalism or graffiti. They explained, however, that they responded very quickly when problems occurred. As one principal explained, "Often, we're able to fix the problem before students or parents notice."

It is important to note that, while a few of the high-performing urban schools we studied were in new or recently constructed buildings, most were not. However, all were maintained in a manner that communicated positive regard for the students in attendance. In many cases, the physical structure conveyed the message that the adults in charge cared enough to create and maintain an environment worthy of the very best students.

One of the best examples of a powerfully positive physical environment is Maplewood Richmond Heights High School in St. Louis, Missouri. Even though most of the building was constructed many years ago, administrators have refurbished the site with attractive display cases featuring artifacts of student accomplishments, meeting rooms that look more like board rooms than urban classrooms, and exposed wood features (e.g., shelves, window frames, and even fireplaces) similar to what one might find in a private university. Students at Maplewood Richmond Heights High know they are valued and capable, in part because the walls remind them every day (Uline & Tschannen-Moran, 2008).

Summary

A student at Park Place Elementary in Houston, Texas, described his school as "a place you can call home." Ultimately, in the high-performing schools we studied, teachers made students feel like they belonged. Without regard to race, ethnicity, family income, language background, immigrant status, gender, disability status, sexual orientation, prior educational success, or any other demographic variable, students perceived that the school they attended was a place where educators cared about them and valued them enough to transform the school into a place where they could and would succeed. By generating this sense of belonging, educators built a powerful foundation for the school's academic success. Chapters 2 through 8 describe other important teaching practices found in these successful schools; however, the practices described in this chapter are at the heart of each school's success.

What It Is & What It Isn't

Making Students Feel Valued and Capable

✓ What It Is

Caring enough to know and value individual students

> Example: During passing periods, the art teacher stands at the door and greets students as they walk by. The teacher's quiet, sincere, and personalized greetings and questions help students know that the teacher cares about them individually.

> Example: A team of teachers and paraprofessionals identify a list of students who are not known well by the school personnel. Each team member takes five students from the list and agrees to make deliberate efforts to get to know the student and a person from the student's family during the semester. In collaboration meetings, the team members share what they have learned about their students.

✗ What It Isn't

Missing opportunities to let students know that educators value them individually

> Example: During passing periods, the art teacher stands at the door and does not say anything as students pass by, except to tell students to hurry to their next class.

> Example: An educator spends considerable time preparing lessons, but does so with little or no information about the interests, situations, strengths, and needs of the students in her classroom.

✓ What It Is

Caring enough to model courtesy and respect

> Example: The fifth-grade teacher asks the students to please turn in their homework. Without warning, one of the students yells out, "Bitch!" The teacher calmly finishes giving directions to the class and then walks back to Mark (the student who made the remark) and whispers for him to follow her into the hall. When the two are in the hallway, the teacher asks, "What was that about?" Mark answers, "I just got a text from my grandmother." Mark shows his cell phone to the teacher, and she sees the text message explaining that Mark's mom was back in jail. "This is the third time she's been in jail," Mark explains with tears rolling down his cheeks. "I'm sorry to hear about your mom," the teacher says. The two of them talk for a minute, and then the teacher asks if Mark needs more time to get himself together. "No. I'm OK," he decides. "So, am I going to have to stay for after-school detention?" Mark asks,

before he opens the classroom door. "Absolutely," the teacher responds. "You broke a rule. But, it will be OK. The detention will give you time to work on some math skills."

(X) What It Isn't

Missing opportunities to demonstrate courtesy and respect to students

Example: The fifth-grade teacher asks the students to please turn in their homework. Without warning, one of the students yells out, "Bitch!" The teacher yells back, "If you didn't do your homework, it's your own fault. How dare you call me a name! Get out of my classroom and march yourself down to the office. I don't care if they never let you come back!"

(✓) What It Is

Caring enough to praise and acknowledge

Example: As the teacher works with seven first-grade students at the reading table, she comments, "I love the way the Princeton group is working quietly together. And I really appreciate the way the Stanford group is following directions. And my San Diego State group, you are reading so well together. What great scholars we have!" Then, the teacher returns her focus to the group at the reading table. Every five minutes or so, she takes the opportunity to notice and comment on the positive things students are doing at their learning centers. Her positive comments seem to fuel their interest in staying on task.

(X) What It Isn't

Missing opportunities to praise and acknowledge

Example: As the teacher works with seven first-grade students at the reading table, she does not notice that the other students are attending to their learning center tasks fairly well. After a while, however, the students are less focused, and eventually they become loud and disruptive. The teacher raises her voice to tell students to lower theirs, but that still does not work, so the teacher ends the guided reading lesson early.

(✓) What It Is

Caring enough to demand the best from students

Example: Even though they recognize the next topic on the district's scope and sequence chart as critically important, the middle school math department members acknowledge that it might be impossible to get their sixth-grade students to master the topic in the three days allotted. They determine that approximately 65 percent of their students are two years behind grade level in math. They challenge themselves to determine what students need to know and be able to do in order to master the concept in a way that would meet the grade-level expectation. Then they determine that they would have a reasonable chance of getting all, or almost all, of their students to this level of mastery if they spent eight days teaching it. Next, they determine the less critical concepts they could remove from "their school's version" of the scope and sequence chart, freeing up the eight days they need to teach this important skill well. Following the eight days of focused instruction, students knew they had accomplished grade-level work. They were proud of themselves. Several expressed that they liked this kind of math. Some talked about how they could be good at math after all.

(X) What It Isn't

Holding students to lower behavioral and academic expectations because of the challenges in their lives

Example: Even though they recognize the next topic on the district's scope and sequence chart as critically important, the middle school math department members acknowledge that it might be impossible to get their sixth-grade students to master the topic in the three days allotted. They determine that approximately 65 percent of their students are two years behind grade level in math, so they decide to focus on a three-day sequence of lessons that would advance the students slightly by teaching the fourth-grade application of the concept. After the three days, some students could be heard complaining about the "baby work" they received in math. Teachers were frustrated with the students' general lack of mastery. Some students stopped trying. Everyone moved on to the next topic in the scope and sequence.

(✓) What It Is

Caring enough to transform educational practices

Example: The biology teachers notice that most of the students who fail their end-of-course test are students with disabilities. The biology teachers consult with the district's best special educators to identify a set of teaching strategies that should help students with disabilities (as well as other students) master the biology content. They work with the special education teacher at their school to "frontload" key biology vocabulary. In other words, the special education teacher helps introduce the key vocabulary words prior to their introduction in the biology class. Also, with the help of school administrators, the biology teachers organize an after-school biology club, and they encourage the participation of all students but offer personal invitations to students with disabilities. The club provides practical, fun experiences through which students utilize important biology concepts. After planning this series of actions, the teachers decide how they will monitor the progress of all students, especially students with disabilities, as they work to learn the key biology concepts.

(X) What It Isn't

Settling for minimal levels of academic progress

> Example: The biology teachers notice that most of the students who fail their end-of-course test are students with disabilities. They decide to use a lower passing score in grading the end-of-course tests for students with disabilities.

(✓) What It Is

Caring enough to create attractive and educationally rich physical environments

> Example: The eighth-grade English classes meet in an old portable building on the east end of the campus. Students call the classroom the Writers' Corner because that is the name on the address plaque over the front door. Volunteer students and former students painted the exterior walls with murals of a group of famous artists who represent both genders and various racial/ethnic groups. The same group of volunteers planted sod and flower gardens in ways that make Writers' Corner an attractive place. On one side of the classroom, sofas, love seats, beanbags, and other chairs create the Readers' Circle. On the other end of the classroom, tables and chairs are clustered to facilitate group writing projects. Short bookshelves line the room, filled with a modest collection of interesting reading material. A portable computer lab, with laptop computers, provides easy access to computers and printers. The largest bulletin board in the classroom is the Honor Board. The Honor Board is filled with student writing products that met rigorous criteria. These examples of student work are attractively posted with the scoring guide and teacher comments associated with each project. The contents of the Honor Board are changed each month. Students work hard to ensure that they always have at least one piece of work on the Honor Board. Another wall features the names, pictures, and college affiliations of recent graduates who had been Writers' Corner participants and now attend colleges or universities. A third wall features computer-generated book jackets. When students read books and complete book reports, they generate the book jacket, post it, and sign the inside cover. As other students

read the book, they can sign the book jacket as well. A glass display case holds the self-published books students from the current and previous classes have written. Students can check out, read, and report about these books, just as they can read and report about other volumes in the classroom.

Ⓧ What It Isn't

Missing opportunities to create attractive physical environments

Example: The eighth-grade English classes meet in an old portable building on the east end of the campus. Students call the classroom the school's ghetto. The exterior walls are dirty and dingy. One window was boarded up two years ago and has never been repaired. Graffiti covers the side of the building closest to the street. The floor of the building is always dirty because students track in dirt and mud from the barren ground between the main building and the portable. Except for a few store-bought posters, the fire drill procedure, and a teacher-made chart with consequences for bad student behavior, the interior classroom walls are bare. The redeeming feature of the building is the relatively large square footage. The teacher has taken advantage of the large space by placing the thirty-five desks into a seven-by-five array with plenty of space in between desks. Most students hate being assigned to classes that meet in the ghetto.

Practice Guide Related to Making Students Feel Valued and Capable

For information on possible uses of this practice guide, please see page xiii in the Preface.

Create a map of the classroom with all of the student seats. Draw a circle to represent each student.

1. Throughout the observation draw a plus sign in a student's circle if the teacher has an interaction with the student that is likely to result in the student feeling more valued and or capable. Draw a minus sign in a student's circle if the teacher has an interaction with the student that is likely to result in the student feeling less valued and or capable. Be careful to code interactions as pluses or minuses based on how you think the student felt (not based on what might have the teacher's intent).

2. Review the data in collaboration with the teacher.

   a. What patterns did you observe? Are there patterns related to race? gender? language background?

b. Which students had many plus signs?

c. Which students had many negative signs?

d. Which students did not have any interactions at all?

e. What might have been missed opportunities for the teacher to make more students feel valued and capable (especially for students with negative interactions or no interactions with the teacher)?

Practical Next Steps

1. In collaboration with teacher colleagues, review your list of students and determine which students you know best and which students you know least. Select four that you will commit to learning more about in the coming month. For each of your four selected students, create a list of strategies you will use to get to know more about them. The strategies might include things such as the following:

   A. Call home, introducing yourself to the student's parents and expressing your aspirations for the student's success.

   B. Create a list of questions that you might ask during one-to-one conversations with students (e.g., What do you like most about school? What do you like least? Where did you go to school before you came here? What is your favorite TV show and why?)

   C. During the school day, observe your selected students and ask, "If I were this student, would I feel valued in this class? Why or why not? Would I feel capable?"

2. Invite a colleague to observe you teaching. Ask the colleague to provide honest feedback regarding the following:

   A. What you did well that probably helped your students feel valued and capable

   B. What you could have done more that would increase the likelihood that your students feel valued and capable

   C. What you did that might have led some students to feel that they were not valued or capable

   D. Were there differences in how you treated/responded to students from different racial/ethnic groups?

3. Observe a colleague who tends to achieve positive learning results for diverse populations of students. While observing, note both the subtle and the obvious things the teacher does to increase the extent

to which diverse groups of students are likely to feel valued and capable. Choose two strategies to practice in your classroom.

4. Utilize the two-by-ten strategy for building relationships with students (see Fisher et al., 2018). First, in collaboration with your colleagues, list the names of students who have not benefitted from strong positive relationships with staff members. Second, each staff member selects a few of the identified students and agrees to spend time developing a relationship with those students. Specifically, each staff member commits to dedicating two minutes each day for ten consecutive days in conversation with the selected students. For the first ten days, the conversations can cover any topic other than school or work. After the ten days, the conversation can address any topic of mutual interest, including school or work.

References

Bondy, E., & Ross, D. D. (2008). The teacher as warm demander. *Educational Leadership, 66*(1), 54–58.

Duncan-Andrade, J. (2009). Note to educators: Hope required when growing roses in concrete. *Harvard Educational Review, 79*(2), 181–194.

Fisher, D., Frey, N., Quaglia, R. J., Smith, D., & Lande, L. L. (2018). *Engagement by design: Creating learning environments where students thrive*. Thousand Oaks, CA: Corwin.

Ferguson, R. (2002). *What doesn't meet the eye: Understanding and addressing racial disparities in high-achieving suburban schools*. Oak Brook, IL: North Central Regional Educational Lab.

Gonzalez, M. L. (2015). *Latino males and academic achievement* (Doctoral dissertation), San Diego State University, San Diego, CA.

Hattie, J. (2009). *Visible learning: A synthesis of over 800 meta-analyses relating to achievement*. New York, NY: Routledge.

Irvine, J. J., & Fraser, J. W. (1998). Warm demanders. *Education Week, 17*(35), 56.

Johnson, J. F., Uline, C. L., & Perez, L. (2017). *Leadership in America's best urban schools*. New York: Routledge and Taylor & Francis Group.

Klem, A. M., & Connell, J. P. (2004). Relationships matter: Linking teacher support to student engagement and achievement. *Journal of School Health, 74*(7), 262–273.

Ladson-Billings, G. (2002). I ain't writin' nuttin': Permissions to fail and demands to succeed in urban classrooms. In L. Depit & J. K. Dowdy (Eds.), *The skin that we speak: Thoughts on language and culture in the classroom* (pp. 107–120). New York: The New Press.

Noddings, N. (1984). *Caring: A feminine approach to ethics and moral education*. Berkeley: University of California Press.

Noddings, N. (2005). *The challenge to care in schools: An alternative approach to education* (2nd ed.). New York: Teachers College Press.

Scheurich, J. J. (1998). Highly successful and loving, public elementary schools populated mainly by low-SES children of color: Core beliefs and cultural characteristics. *Urban Education, 33*(4), 451–491.

Uline, C. L., & Tschannen-Moran, M. (2008). The walls speak: The interplay of quality facilities, school climate, and student achievement. *Journal of Educational Administration, 46*, 55–73.

Uline, C. L., Tschannen-Moran, M., & Wolsey, T. D. (2009). The walls still speak: The stories occupants tell. *Journal of Educational Administration, 47*, 400–426.

Valenzuela, A. (1999). *Subtractive schooling: U.S.-Mexican youth and the politics of caring.* Albany: SUNY Press.

2

Focusing on Understanding and Mastery

A science teacher at Horace Mann Dual Language Academy in Wichita, Kansas, explained (in Spanish) to her class of fifth-grade students that during the class period they would learn five concepts related to volcanic activity. She explained that by the end of the period, they would be able to describe (in Spanish) each of the five concepts and explain how the concepts were related. Immediately, she asked several students to describe (in Spanish) what they were going to learn during the lesson. Next, using Spanish vocabulary the students had previously mastered, the teacher explained each concept. Immediately after each explanation, she asked several students to explain the concept in their own words (in Spanish). After several students had explained each concept and students seemed fairly comfortable with the new vocabulary, the teacher invited pairs of students to come to the front of the room and pantomime a concept. Other students were expected to guess which concept the students were modeling. Every student was paying attention to the pantomimes, trying to be one of the first to guess the intended meaning. As students became more comfortable using the new vocabulary, the teacher asked additional questions that required students to explain the relationships among the concepts. The teacher asked questions of every student. If a student did not know the answer, the teacher asked another student but within a few minutes returned to the initial student with the same question. In this way, each student felt responsible for paying attention and learning the content, even if they could not respond to the teacher's initial question. By the end of the lesson, students were using the new Spanish vocabulary comfortably. Students asked questions about important details. The teacher used those questions to deepen the conversation and teach more about volcanic activity. At the end of the period, as students left the classroom, the researcher stopped a few students and asked them what they had learned in class. In English, they explained the concepts they had learned, accurately and with impressive detail.

Horace Mann Dual Language Academy is in the Wichita Public School District in Wichita, Kansas. The school serves approximately 530 students in grades kindergarten through eight. The school won the America's Best Urban Schools Award in 2009.

A Perpetual Question

On the Minds of Educators Striving to Produce Equity and Excellence

How can I get each and every one of my students to believe, "My teacher wants me to understand this well enough to use it throughout my life and my teacher is wise enough and relentless enough to guide me so I will master it"?

Many U.S. teachers perceive that their job is to prepare and present a series of academic lessons, covering specific topics and specific academic standards, across

Figure 2.1

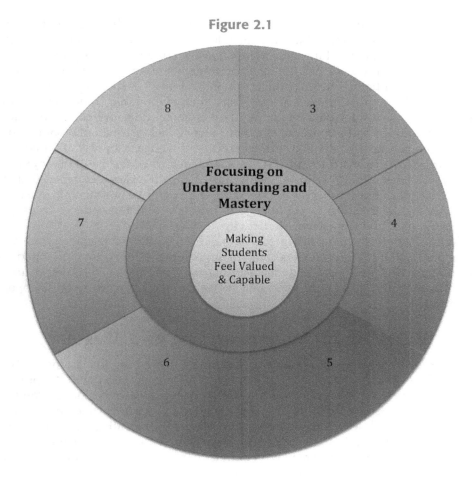

an academic year. Of course, teachers are expected to fulfill this responsibility while simultaneously managing classroom and school routines, student behavior, paper-work, and other assorted duties; however, school districts and teacher-training institutions have led teachers to perceive that their job is primarily to organize and present academic content.

In contrast, we found a profound, albeit subtle, difference in the way teachers in high-performing urban schools perceived their work. These teachers acted as if their job was to ensure that their students understood specific academic content and skills with sufficient depth that allowed students to utilize the content and skills to solve problems and/or better understand their world. For these teachers, presenting or covering content was not the goal. Instead, they focused upon leading students—all of their students—to understand important concepts and demonstrate mastery of specific academic objectives. They persistently, and sometimes relentlessly, worked to ensure that each of their students achieved a depth of understanding. Teachers approached each lesson with a sense of mission. The mission was not to follow the teacher's guide, cover the chapter, or even present the relevant content. Instead, the mission was to help every student achieve a level of understanding sufficient to lead to mastery. As illustrated by Figure 2.1, the focus on understanding and mastery contributed to students feeling valued and capable. As well, the focus on understanding and mastery was enhanced through attention to each of the other six practices.

It is important to note that the focus on understanding and mastery for every student is substantially different from traditional approaches that suggest the teacher's job is to distinguish "those who can" from "those who can't." Bloom (1971) considered a focus on understanding and mastery as an antidote for bell-curve notions of student aptitude and achievement and one-size-fits-all instruction. Bloom argued that we can get most students to master content if we teach in ways that address their learning needs. More recently, Guskey (2007) described the use of Bloom's mastery approach as a tool for closing achievement gaps. Guskey explained that the positive effects of mastery learning extend beyond cognitive or academic outcomes to improvements in students' confidence as learners, school attendance rates, and attitudes toward and engagement in learning.

In the high-performing urban schools studied, we found teachers who were convinced that all of their students could demonstrate mastery if they provided lessons that responded to their students' learning strengths and needs. Their focus on understanding and mastery resulted in achievement gaps narrowing or disappearing entirely.

Planning for Understanding and Mastery

After forty-five years of research on teaching and learning in classrooms, Nuthall (2005) concluded that many teachers do not plan instruction with the purpose of ensuring that their students achieve mastery. Instead, teachers tend to plan with focus more on keeping students busy and carrying out routines. In contrast, in the schools we studied, lesson planning was not focused on creating busywork, complying with a principal's mandates, or staying in step with a school district's pacing chart. Instead, we found teachers who planned strategically how they would lead the specific students in their classrooms to understand and master specific concepts and skills. The goal of planning was not coverage. Instead, the goal was to provide learning experiences that were likely to result in every student understanding and mastering specific concepts and skills.

A sign in the teachers' lounge area at Bonnie Brae Elementary in the Fort Worth Independent School District reads, "Make a shift from . . . 'I taught it' to 'Did they learn it?'" At Bonnie Brae and many other high-performing urban schools, teachers planned instruction with the explicit intention of ensuring that all their students would understand and master important concepts.

For example, the science teacher at Horace Mann Dual Language Academy (described in the chapter opening) planned to ensure that her students would exit her classroom with a working knowledge of the five concepts she planned to teach that day. She was not content simply to cover pages in a textbook, provide a lecture, or show a video clip. She wanted to be sure that her students would understand each of the key concepts she wanted them to learn. She wanted to be sure that all of her students could discuss the concepts accurately, with some depth of understanding. She wanted to know that each and every student could distinguish among the concepts, describe, explain, compare, and contrast in Spanish! Her goal was mastery, not coverage.

Because the goal of planning was student understanding and mastery, teachers planned with their students in mind. Teachers considered, "What do my students need to see, do, hear, touch, and experience in order to understand and master this important concept?" Teachers considered the prior knowledge, backgrounds, and interests of their students. They considered the vocabulary students might have previously mastered and the vocabulary students were less likely to know well. They considered how textbooks and workbooks might help them guide their students toward understanding and mastery, but they also considered where published materials might fall short and other teaching aids, metaphors, manipulatives, technology, or experiences might help their students develop understanding and achieve mastery of the important academic concepts and skills they sought to teach.

Wiggins and McTighe (2005) encourage educators to focus less on "covering" content and more on planning lessons that lead students to master important content. They contended, "The job of teaching is to optimize student learning of what is worthy—not to 'cover' a book, nor to 'teach, test and hope for the best,' irrespective of [learning] results" (p. 314). In the award-winning schools we studied, we consistently found lessons that were planned to lead students to understanding and mastery. For example, at John Quincy Adams Elementary in Dallas, Texas, teachers planned lessons by focusing on the demonstration of learning they expected students to be able to present.

Overwhelmingly, in the high-performing schools we studied, instructional planning was a team activity. Teachers invested substantial amounts of time in working together to plan lessons that would result in all students understanding key concepts and demonstrating mastery. For example, at Patrick Henry Preparatory School (P.S./I.S. 171) in New York City's District 4, teachers worked collaboratively in grade-level teams to discuss and plan effective teaching strategies that would result in measurable student progress on formative assessments. At Hialeah Gardens Middle School in Miami, Florida, teachers meet regularly during common planning times. Together, they carefully examine student data to help them plan lessons that will result in higher levels of understanding and mastery of Florida's state standards. At Americas High School in El Paso's Socorro Independent School District, teams of teachers meet regularly in content-specific professional learning communities. They work together to plan lessons that aim to create lesson clarity, reduce "teacher talk," increase "student talk," and promote critical writing as a means to deepen understanding. In high-performing urban schools, collaborative teacher planning is an engine that accelerates learning, especially among diverse groups of students.

One reason collaborative teacher planning is so pervasive and so impactful within high-performing urban schools is that well-structured teacher collaboration activities help teachers change their beliefs about what they can teach well and what their students can learn well. Saphier, Haley-Speca, and Gower (2008) determined that a focus on mastery begins with teacher beliefs about their students' capacity to learn and their capacity to teach. By working together to understand key academic standards, examine student-learning data, design powerful lessons, and plan effective intervention and enrichment strategies, educators are more likely to learn to appreciate their collective capacity to ensure the learning success of all their students.

Planning for mastery also means planning to determine how mastery will be assessed. In high-performing urban schools, we found that educators worked together to determine how they would assess the extent to which students understood and mastered essential concepts and skills. For example, at the Middle College at the University of North Carolina Greensboro (UNCG), teachers planned rotations in which students were expected to read, write, think, and speak every day in order to demonstrate their understanding of the concepts being taught. At Mary and Frank Yturria Elementary in Brownsville, Texas, teachers met weekly in grade-level meetings to plan lessons and create assessments that would help teachers determine if students truly understood the concepts teachers intended students to learn.

Dufour and Marzano (2011) emphasized that effective collaborative teams planned and utilized formative assessment to make substantial improvements in learning results. True formative assessments provide teachers useful information about the depth of a student's understanding of a specific concept. Results from formative assessments can guide teachers in planning instruction that will result in better understanding and mastery. In contrast, it is much more common for teachers in schools throughout the United States to use multidimensional assessments that provide a single score as an assessment of the learning of several concepts. At schools such as Maplewood Richmond Heights High in St. Louis, Centennial Elementary in Colorado Springs, Fay Herron Elementary in Las Vegas, Magnet Traditional School in Phoenix, Arizona, Mallard Creek High School in Charlotte, North Carolina, and several other high-performing urban schools, the development and use of formative assessments was an important tool in advancing student understanding.

Designing Objective-Driven Lessons

Often, in our visits to high-performing schools, we heard teachers make statements such as, "Before this period ends, you will be able to explain why . . . " or "In today's class, you're going to show me that you know how to . . . " or "Before the bell rings, I expect each one of you to be able to describe the relationship between . . . " or "By 9:15, I want everyone to be able to describe in writing the steps for solving this kind of problem and explain why each step makes sense." Teachers in high-performing urban schools are explicit about what they want their students to learn. Typically, they write and post the specific learning objective that is the focus of instruction. But even more importantly, they talk about the learning objective with students. They help students know specifically, clearly, and explicitly what they should be attempting to learn. For example, throughout MacArthur High School in the Aldine Independent School District (Houston, Texas), teachers post a three-part objective that explains to students (1) what they are going to learn in the lesson, (2) how they are going to learn it, and (3) how they will know they have learned it. At National City Middle School in National City, California, teachers post the learning target for the day and ask students to focus upon the verb. "What are you going to do today?" an English teacher asked, prompting the students to respond, "Analyze." "And, what will you be analyzing?" he continued. "Character personality traits," a student answered before the teacher led students in a discussion of the specific meaning of this objective.

This is starkly different from classrooms in which teachers post "Math—pages 145–147" or "photosynthesis" as an "objective." In such classrooms, teachers let students know about the activity in which they will engage or the topic area they will address; however, students do not necessarily understand specifically what their teacher expects them to learn or understand by the end of the lesson.

It is important to note, however, that no magic occurs when an objective is written and posted in a classroom. We have seen many classrooms where the objective is posted prominently, yet the written objective seems to have little relationship to the instructional activities. In such classrooms, the presentation of the lesson objective is often an act of compliance. In contrast, in high-performing urban schools, the objective (whether posted or not) drives instruction and learning throughout the period.

These objective-driven lessons are also different from lessons in which teachers specify only a broad standard or learning goal. In some cases, a standard or a learning goal might encompass multiple objectives, requiring a sequence of several lessons. For example, a broad standard might require students to understand fractional concepts. This standard could include a vast array of specific objectives, such as identifying fractional parts of a whole, converting improper fractions, and identifying equivalent fractions. Stating the standard or the learning goal might be helpful in giving students a picture of what they should ultimately learn; however, it might not help students understand what they should know or be able to do at the end of the day's lesson. In the highest-performing schools, teachers recognized that they often needed to identify and teach several objectives in order for their students to master a specific standard or learning goal. Teachers explicitly defined the objective they wanted their students to learn at the moment, en route to mastery of challenging standards.

Frequently, in our visits to classrooms, we ask students what they are learning at that particular moment. In many typical urban schools, we hear students respond, "We're reading this story" or "I've got to finish this worksheet" or "I'm supposed to answer these questions." Their answers suggest that their goal is to complete the activity, do the assignment, or follow the routine. In contrast, in high-performing urban schools, students were much more likely to respond that they were learning a specific academic objective: "We're learning how to calculate the volume of a triangular prism" or "We're trying to determine the author's purpose in different kinds of texts" or "We're learning how heat influences the water cycle." In these classes, students knew the lesson objective, often because it was posted and discussed. Teachers engaged students in discussions concerning both what they would learn and why it was important.

It is important to note that in high-performing urban schools, objectives drive lessons. The activities implemented, the questions asked, the examples provided, the materials chosen, and the tasks assigned are heavily influenced by the objective. "Everything I do, from start to finish, is designed to teach my kids the particular objective I need them to learn," a teacher at Benjamin Franklin Elementary in Bakersfield, California, explained. Similarly, the principal of Thomas Henderson Middle School in Richmond, Virginia, insisted, "All of our instructional decisions are purposeful. We don't do things just because the textbook says or because that's the way we taught it last year. We do things to ensure students learn the objective."

In objective-driven lessons, teachers are constantly focused on what they want students to learn and how they want students to demonstrate they have learned it. While teachers attend to the objective, they also focus on how each student is progressing toward learning the objective. Teachers plan, monitor, and adjust their teaching so that there is a high likelihood that all students will master the lesson objective. Similarly, in objective-driven lessons, students are constantly focused on what they should be trying to understand. As a student at Dayton's Business and Technology High School explained, "At this school, teachers make clear to you exactly what you need to be learning. It's not some big mystery. You know what's expected, so you have a good chance to learn."

Generating Depth of Understanding

A focus on mastery implies more than the pursuit of surface-level knowledge. In high-performing urban schools, many lessons were designed to generate a depth of understanding. Students were expected to analyze, explain, discuss, and apply in ways that exhibited mastery of the content. In these schools, superficial recall of facts was insufficient. For example, while many elementary school students may be expected to learn general facts about slavery and the Civil War, students in a social studies class at Charles Lunsford Elementary in Rochester, New York, were expected to assume the role of Abraham Lincoln's speechwriter. They worked in groups to write speeches that offered arguments against slavery, building from Lincoln's personal experiences. These students acquired a much greater understanding of both the personal history of Lincoln and the impact of slavery on human lives.

Arguably, teaching toward a depth of understanding may take more time than pursuing recall of general facts. Teachers in some schools may perceive that they do not have sufficient time to pursue depth. In high-performing urban schools, we found it common for principals to encourage teachers to pursue depth, even if it meant covering fewer topics (less breadth). Also, teachers in some of these schools reported that their students were less likely to forget concepts and skills when they took the time to pursue a depth of understanding. As a result, teachers could spend less time repeating and reviewing.

In mathematics instruction in high-performing urban schools, we found depth reflected in teaching that required students to answer "Why?" For example, students were not simply asked to "solve for X." They were also asked to explain why each step made sense. They were asked to explain what *solving for* X meant. They were asked to explain why their errors did not make sense. They were asked to apply their knowledge to real situations.

In high-performing urban schools, lesson objectives often specified the depth of knowledge the teacher wanted the students to acquire. For example, objectives might have specified that students would describe, explain, model, demonstrate, debate, justify, construct, or analyze. Accordingly, lessons were organized and presented in ways that were clearly intended to ensure that students would be able to demonstrate the depth of knowledge expected. So, if the objective suggested that students would model a concept, lesson activities were structured in a way that required students to model—and allowed the teacher to determine if students could, in fact, model—the concept. Teachers did not merely present information and hope that students would attain the desired depth of knowledge.

Maximizing Time on Objective

As teachers in high-performing urban schools strive to help students master challenging academic content, they act as if every available minute is a precious resource. They rarely stray from the central concept or skill they are attempting to teach. They might approach the concept in different ways, use different examples, or teach different algorithms; however, they remain focused on the main concept or skill they want students to master.

Within high-performing urban schools, educators have worked together to find ways to minimize distractions. Intercom announcements, bells, and phone distractions have been curtailed or eliminated. Few if any students are pulled out of classrooms because special instructional personnel more typically work alongside the classroom teacher, within the regular classroom setting. Teachers and leaders have worked to minimize transition times and eliminate the time students spend waiting for instruction to commence. Routines are finely tuned so that the maximum amount of time possible can be devoted to learning.

In more typical schools, educators might focus upon maximizing time on task: the time students spend working on an assigned task. Time on task, however, can be maximized with "filler" activities and busywork. In contrast, in high-performing urban schools, teachers are more focused on maximizing the amount of time students spend learning and mastering specific academic objectives. We did not observe students spending large amounts of time copying information, coloring, or completing tasks that required minimal thinking. Often, lesson objectives required students to engage in higher-level thinking processes such as describing, analyzing, comparing, explaining, or evaluating, so lesson activities frequently engaged students in dialogue that encouraged these mental activities. Of course, there were times when students copied information or colored pictures; however, in high-performing urban schools, those types of activities consumed a much smaller percentage of time compared to the percentage of time they consume in typical urban schools.

In high-performing urban schools, lessons rarely end before the class period ends. Teachers eagerly use minutes at the end of the period to check to ensure that students have mastered the objective taught. From start to finish, each lesson fills the available time, not simply because teachers are complying with administrative demands but because teachers want to ensure that true understanding and mastery have occurred.

Focusing on All Students

Teachers in the high-performing schools studied were not content to see a few or several students understand and master the content they attempted to teach. They insisted upon high levels of engagement from all students because they wanted every student to understand key concepts and exhibit mastery. At Marble Hill High School for International Studies in the Bronx, New York, teachers asserted that they never gave up on a student. One teacher explained, "In our school, we just don't give up . . . as long as a problem continues, we will continue to address it."

In more typical urban schools, we found classrooms where teachers seemed satisfied if students looked as if they were paying attention. In some classrooms, teachers seemed to be pleased if students were simply not being disruptive. In some classrooms of twenty, twenty-five, thirty, or more students, teachers provided a monologue or engaged in dialogue with only one or two students, while other students sat quietly, some with vacant expressions, some with their heads on their desks, some reading material completely unrelated to the lesson, and even some sleeping.

In contrast, in high-performing urban schools, teachers refused to allow students to sit passively and fail to learn. Teachers insisted that all students participate, engage, think, discuss, contribute, and make academic progress. Much of the substance of the following six chapters explains how teachers created classroom environments in which student engagement was likely. In other words, teachers employed a variety of cognitive and affective practices that maximized the likelihood of active student participation.

While examining the subsequent chapters, keep in mind that teachers in these high-performing schools were particularly eager to ensure the engagement of groups of students who traditionally have not achieved well. For example, teachers were particularly deliberate in ensuring the engagement of English learners, students with disabilities, highly mobile students, students with lower reading abilities, and students who had histories of discipline problems. As well, teachers were deliberately focused on ensuring the engagement of students from racial and ethnic groups who historically have been underserved. In particular, we found many schools where teachers overtly discussed and monitored the extent to which African American, Latino, Southeast Asian, and Native American students demonstrated understanding and mastery of key learning objectives. In fact, students from these groups often made substantial and sometimes dramatic academic gains because their teachers made persistent, conscientious, multipronged efforts to generate a high level of engagement among students who often become invisible in more typical urban schools.

In almost all of the high-performing urban schools we visited, students with mild or moderate disabilities received special services primarily in their regular classrooms. For example, at Louisa May Alcott in Cleveland, Ohio, special education personnel worked alongside general classroom teachers to help ensure that students with disabilities achieved the same academic results expected for all students. At Jim Thorpe Fundamental School in Santa Ana, California, special educators assumed responsibility for helping ensure that students with disabilities mastered the objectives that other students were being taught. Typically, special educators provided services in general education classrooms. Even when students with disabilities did not master the objective, they showed evidence of important academic gains that placed them closer to grade-level expectations. Special education was made "special" by the intensity of the effort to get students to master the general education curriculum. Specialists worked in collaboration with general education teachers to plan and implement a quality of services that led many students with disabilities to achieve grade-level proficiency.

In some schools, like Stephens Elementary in Houston, Texas (Aldine Independent School District), many English learners were served in separate bilingual classes; however, we consistently observed the teachers in the bilingual classes pursuing the same academic objectives with the same level of rigor as observed in classrooms taught exclusively in English. Bilingual education was not a separate track with different academic goals. Instead, bilingual classes offered a parallel route to the same high academic expectations held for all students throughout the school.

Similarly, at Nathan Adams Elementary in Dallas, Texas, native Spanish-speaking students and native English-speaking students learned the same content, read the same books, and did the same work at the same high levels of achievement, regardless of the language of instruction. The language of instruction is a tool for ensuring that all students achieve high levels of academic success.

Summary

This pursuit of understanding and mastery for all students is central to teaching in high-performing urban schools. The other practices discussed in this book all contribute to the effort to generate high levels of engagement, understanding, and mastery among all students. Specifically, the mastery-oriented practices we observed included efforts to present lessons in a logical, clear, and concise manner (Chapter 3); connect lesson objectives with students' interests, backgrounds, cultures, and prior knowledge (Chapter 4); check understanding and provide feedback (Chapter 5); make the lesson vocabulary part of students' conversational vocabulary (Chapter 6); promote practice opportunities that were likely to build and reinforce academic success (Chapter 7); and provide lessons that were interesting and stimulating so that students were likely to learn to love learning (Chapter 8).

Ultimately, the focus on understanding and mastery is more than a teaching practice. It is the attitude, the orientation, the sense of urgency, the reason for teaching we noticed as we entered classrooms and observed teachers and students interact. Perhaps the best way of describing this focus was offered several years before we began our current study. In 1998, the principal of Brazosport High School in Brazosport, Texas, was interviewed in a study of high-performing schools. Achievement results had improved dramatically and earned the school an exemplary rating in the state's accountability system. The principal, Mr. Boone, was asked to describe the primary differences between his school then and his school several years prior, when the school's academic results had been dismal. After pondering a few moments, the principal replied, "Well, back then [prior to the school's improvement], we taught school like we were feeding the chickens." When the interviewer asked for clarification, the principal gave the following explanation:

> When you feed the chickens, you strap on your bag of feed and go out into the yard and toss the feed onto the ground. If the chickens eat the feed, that's fine. If they don't, that's fine. Your job is just to toss it out there. That's the way we taught school. We strapped on our lesson plans, we went into our classrooms, and we tossed out the information. If the students got it, fine. If the students didn't get it, fine. Back then, we thought our job was just to present the information, to toss it out there. The difference now is that our teachers want to see evidence that students have taken it in, ingested it, and digested the information. We don't stop until we see evidence that students have understood what we want them to learn. That's the main difference between our school back then and our school today.

Similarly, one might say that this is the main difference between schools with a focus on mastery and other schools. In the high-performing schools we awarded and studied, consistently we saw teachers who were not satisfied to present the material, follow the lesson plan, pass out the worksheets, or otherwise "toss the feed." Instead, they were determined to ensure that students learned, absorbed, understood, and applied the specific objective of their lesson.

What It Is & What It Isn't

Focusing on Understanding and Mastery

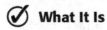 What It Is

Focusing on getting students to understand specific content or skills

> Example: The objective posted on the board read, "Students will make and justify logical inferences based upon nonfiction, grade-level text." At the beginning of the lesson, the teacher discussed the objective with the students and helped them understand what they should be able to do by the lesson's end. At various points during the lesson, the teacher reminded students that they were becoming more skillful at making and justifying logical inferences. Throughout the lesson, the teacher asked questions and posed tasks designed to get students to demonstrate their understanding of the concept of inference. As well, the teacher's questions helped her understand how well students made and justified inferences based upon the nonfiction, grade-level text they were using.

Ⓧ What It Isn't

Focusing on "covering" a set of concepts, skills, or pages during the period/day/ unit

> Example: The objective posted on the board read, "Inferences." While the teacher covered information about inferences from the teacher's manual, she never explained the objective to students. She covered the material without ascertaining if students had any understanding of the concept or any ability to make and justify logical inferences.

⊘ What It Is

Planning collaboratively to ensure that students understand and master key academic concepts

> Example: A team of high school biology teachers met to discuss how they would get their students to understand and master concepts that influence how the characteristics of one generation are passed to the next. Team members worked together to define what students would need to understand in order to achieve the level of mastery they expected. Utilizing their definition of mastery, the teachers created formative assessments that would help them gauge student progress. Before the teachers planned a series of lessons, they looked at the results from assessments given in prior years. Together, they considered what concepts were difficult to teach and thought about the factors that might have impeded

student understanding (e.g., difficult vocabulary, potentially confusing concepts, challenging texts). Then they worked collaboratively to create model lessons intended to increase the likelihood that students would understand and master the key concepts. The teachers even created sample questions they could ask students throughout the lessons to determine if students truly understood the key concepts.

(X) What It Isn't

Planning solo with the hope that one's planning ability will be better than it was the prior year

Example: The biology department chair announced that lesson plans for the genetics unit were due on Friday afternoon. Each biology teacher, working in isolation, took time at home or during their planning period to plan lessons. Some biology teachers found last year's genetics lessons and made a few cosmetic adjustments.

(✓) What It Is

Structuring lesson activities to maximize the likelihood that students will learn the lesson objective (creating objective-driven lessons)

Example: The teacher engaged students in three different learning centers while she provided guided instruction to a fourth group of students. The guided instruction and the activities in two of the three learning centers focused on sequencing events in expository text. The fourth center provided students an opportunity to practice a literacy skill they had developed during a previous instructional unit. To prepare the guided instruction and the two learning centers focused on sequencing events, the teacher worked with colleagues to review common student errors related to sequencing events described in expository texts. This preparation helped the teachers develop questions to guide students away from common misconceptions (e.g., the first event mentioned in the text should be sequenced first) and helped students develop strategies for more accurately determining the sequence of events. The planning also helped the teachers develop center activities that would allow students to practice strategies in small groups. Throughout the lesson, the teacher tried to monitor the extent to which students were understanding and implementing the strategies well. In particular, during guided instruction, the teacher listened closely to student explanations of their answers to ensure that they understood the concept of sequencing events well. If necessary, the teacher was prepared to modify questions, examples, or explanations to maximize the likelihood that students would understand how to sequence events with great accuracy.

Ⓧ What It Isn't

Working to "cover" a variety of topics, while devoting only a small fraction of time, thought, and energy to the concept/skill the teacher wants students to understand

> Example: The teacher engaged students in four different learning centers, each focused on a different objective, while she provided guided instruction to a small group on another objective. The teacher prepared the guided instruction using the same materials, examples, and questions she used last year when only half of the students demonstrated that they could sequence events accurately.

Ⓥ What It Is

Aiming to get students to demonstrate a thorough, deep understanding of a concept or skill

> Example: The teacher focused upon getting students to explain *why* a common algorithm worked when they added fractions with unlike denominators. The teacher was not satisfied that students could find the least common denominator or determine equivalent fractions. She wanted to hear students explain why the algorithm works. She organized students into teams and gave each team the responsibility of teaching the class why the algorithm they learned works when adding fractions with unlike denominators. She provided each team with a variety of manipulatives, chart paper, and marking pens. She listened attentively as students worked to create explanations. To ensure that students truly understood, occasionally, the teacher interjected, "Why does that make sense?"

Ⓧ What It Isn't

Aiming to get students to demonstrate a surface-level understanding

> Example: The teacher focused upon getting students to solve problems involving the addition of fractions with unlike denominators. If students answered 80 percent of the problems correctly, the teacher assumed that students understood and mastered the objective.

Ⓥ What It Is

Maximizing time students spend developing understanding of the lesson objective

> Example: The geometry teachers planned a lesson to teach students how to find the volume of spheres, cylinders, and cones. As the teacher listened to student responses, she realized that some students were confusing strategies for finding the volume of these objects with strategies for finding the volume of various polygonal prisms. She modified the lesson by creating a T-chart on the front

board. On the left side of the T-chart, she drew pictures of different polygonal prisms and asked students to describe the strategy for finding the volume of each. Then, on the right side, she drew examples of spheres, cylinders, and cones. When she asked students how to find the volume of these solid shapes, students began to see that they were applying the same strategies they used for polygonal prisms. "Why would the formula for finding the volume of a cylinder be different from the formula for finding the volume of a rectangular prism?" she asked. Students explained that the size of a round base is likely to be different than the size of a rectangular base. With this "aha!" moment, students began to understand the distinctions in the formulae.

(X) What It Isn't

Maximizing time on task vaguely connected to the objective

Example: The geometry teacher planned a lesson to teach students how to find the volume of spheres, cylinders, and cones. The teacher motored through the lesson as planned, even though some students seemed to confuse strategies for finding the volume of these solid objects with strategies for finding the volume of polygonal prisms. The teacher then filled the remainder of the class period by engaging students in creating paper models of spheres, cylinders, cones, cubes, and various polygonal prisms.

(✓) What It Is

Expecting each and every student to work toward mastery of challenging objectives, providing support to students who need special assistance, and providing enrichment opportunities that keep students feeling challenged.

Example: The teacher planned lesson activities in consideration of her students' wide range of abilities. When she recognized that some students were having difficulty completing the assignment independently, she provided intensive assistance designed to help them understand. On the other hand, she gave students who completed the assignment early a "may do" assignment that required them to pursue the objective at a deeper level.

(X) What It Isn't

Expecting students with specific learning needs to pursue different, lesser, and often unrelated learning objectives and expecting students who demonstrate success quickly to sit and wait

Example: The teacher planned one major lesson activity for all students. Students who had difficulty completing the assignment (because they did not understand the content) turned in blank papers. Students who completed the assignment early were expected to sit quietly.

Practice Guide Related to Focusing on Understanding and Mastery

For information on possible uses of this practice guide, please see page xiii in the Preface.

Table 2.1

1.	Is there substantial evidence that students understand what they are supposed to know and be able to do as a result of the lesson?	Ⓨ	Ⓝ
	A. Is there evidence that students in every demographic group understand what they are supposed to know and be able to do as a result of the lesson?	Ⓨ	Ⓝ
	B. Is there evidence that students of varying academic abilities understand what they are supposed to know and be able to do as a result of the lesson?		
2.	Was the lesson objective influencing the teacher's actions throughout the lesson? (Did the objective—not the textbook, a worksheet, or a teacher's manual—drive the lesson?)	Ⓨ	Ⓝ
3.	If an observer asked students to describe the objective being taught, could each student offer an appropriate description?	Ⓨ	Ⓝ
4.	At various times throughout the lesson, did the teacher remind students of the objective being taught?	Ⓨ	Ⓝ
5.	Were all or almost all lesson activities/discussions focused on the lesson objective?	Ⓨ	Ⓝ
6.	Did lesson activities reflect careful planning intended to result in students' mastering the specific objective?	Ⓨ	Ⓝ
7.	Did the lesson require students to use higher cognitive skills than recall or memorization?	Ⓨ	Ⓝ
8.	Were the lesson activities designed to help students achieve the depth of knowledge articulated in the lesson objective?	Ⓨ	Ⓝ
9.	Did the lesson occur without significant distractions?	Ⓨ	Ⓝ
10.	Were transition times minimized?	Ⓨ	Ⓝ
11.	Were more than 90 percent of the students focused on the objective at least 90 percent of the time?	Ⓨ	Ⓝ
12.	Are at least 50 percent of the students likely to show mastery of the content taught during the lesson?	Ⓨ	Ⓝ
13.	Are at least 75 percent of the students likely to show mastery of the content taught during the lesson?	Ⓨ	Ⓝ
14.	Are at least 90 percent of the students likely to show mastery of the content taught during the lesson?	Ⓨ	Ⓝ

In a strong lesson, a "yes" answer is recorded for at least eight of these items.
In an outstanding lesson, a "yes" answer is recorded for at least twelve of these items.

Practical Next Steps

1. In collaboration with teacher colleagues, engage in a book study of *Leaders of Learning* (Dufour & Marzano, 2011). If time does not allow a focus on the entire book, pay specific attention to Chapters 4, 5, and 6.
2. In collaboration with teacher colleagues, engage in a book study of *Understanding by Design* (Wiggins & McTighe, 2005). If time does not allow a focus on the entire book, pay specific attention to Chapters 1, 2, and 3.
3. In collaboration with teacher colleagues (individuals who teach the same subject area and/or the same grade level), identify a major learning objective that, in recent years, many students at your school have not mastered. Select a concept or set of concepts that you will not need to begin teaching immediately. (Ideally, if this is your first time planning together, you should have two to four weeks of planning time before you begin teaching the content.)
4. Schedule a series of meeting times with teacher colleagues. The planning meetings should occur at least once a week. Ensure that everyone will be in attendance at the planning meetings, including teachers and support staff who share responsibility for educating students with disabilities, English learners, or other students with special needs.
5. As a team, begin planning by establishing a common understanding of what students should be able to do in order to demonstrate real mastery of the learning objective selected. Develop formative assessments that you and your colleagues will use to gauge student progress in understanding.
6. Review assessment results from previous years to learn what students understood well and what they didn't understand as a result of the instruction provided. Identify common misconceptions and consider what might have influenced those misconceptions.
7. Work together to establish model lessons that should have a high likelihood of leading all students to understand and master the selected learning objective.
8. Before teaching a lesson, define one small learning outcome that you would like to see every student demonstrate at the end of the lesson. Even if it takes more time than anticipated, try to develop and implement teaching approaches that will result in all students achieving the learning outcome. If necessary, seek ideas from colleagues as you endeavor to ensure understanding and mastery for all students.

References

Bloom, B. S. (1971). Mastery learning. In J. H. Block (Ed.), *Mastery learning: Theory and practice* (pp. 47–63). New York: Holt, Rinehart, & Winston.

Dufour, R., & Marzano, R. J. (2011). *Leaders of learning: How district, school, and classroom leaders improve student achievement*. Bloomington, IN: Solution Tree Press.

Guskey, T. R. (2007, Fall). Closing achievement gaps: Revisiting Benjamin S. Bloom's "learning for mastery". *Journal of Advanced Academics*, 8–31.

Nuthall, G. (2005). The cultural myths and realities of teaching and learning: A personal journey. *Teachers College Record, 107*(5), 895–934.

Saphier, J., Haley-Speca, M. A., & Gower, R. (2008). *The skillful teacher: Building your teaching skills*. Acton, MA: Research for Better Teaching.

Wiggins, G. P., & McTighe, J. (2005). *Understanding by design* (Expanded 2nd ed.). Upper Saddle River, NJ: Pearson Education, Inc.

3

Promoting Clarity

A fifth-grade teacher at Highland Elementary was teaching his students to under-stand linear equations. In a prior lesson, students had learned about variables. In this lesson, the focus was on mathematic expressions. The teacher succinctly explained to students that an algebraic expression combined a variable and a value. He provided a variety of practical examples and then engaged the students in brain-storming many additional examples.

One student offered, "Like the number of points your team gets for a score could be a variable and the number of scores could be the value."

"Yes," the teacher responded. "So, what might an expression be for three scores?"

"Three S," the student answered proudly.

"Exactly! So, what does the expression 'Three S' mean?" the teacher asked a different student.

"It means three times an unknown number," the student answered.

"An unknown number of what?" the teacher probed?

"An unknown number of scores," stated another child.

Students were then directed to list expressions on sentence strips and then, on separate sentence strips, write out words that would indicate what the expressions meant. Later students played a matching game in which they matched the sentence strips by pairing the algebraic expressions with the matching word sentences.

Highland Elementary is in the Montgomery County Public School District in Silver Spring, Maryland. The school serves approximately 450 students in grades pre-kindergarten through five. The school won the America's Best Urban Schools Award in 2009.

A Perpetual Question

On the Minds of Educators Striving to Produce Equity and Excellence

How can I get each and every one of my students to think, "I understand precisely what my teacher wants me to learn and I see how my teacher is leading me toward understanding it"?

Teaching practices influence student understanding, even more than socio-economic factors (Hattie, 2009). Students master more when teachers introduce con-tent with great clarity. Saphier, Haley-Speca, and Gower (2008) insisted, "Skillful teachers are clear about what is to be learned, clear about what achievement means, and clear about what they are going to do to help students attain it" (p. 2).

In high-performing urban schools, teachers enable students to access informa-tion in a manner that facilitates understanding. Teachers plan instruction so that understanding is likely, often without the need for remediation or intervention. As suggested by Figure 3.1, by promoting clarity, teachers focus on getting students to understand and master important concepts. As well, by promoting clarity, teachers increase the likelihood that students feel valued and capable.

Figure 3.1

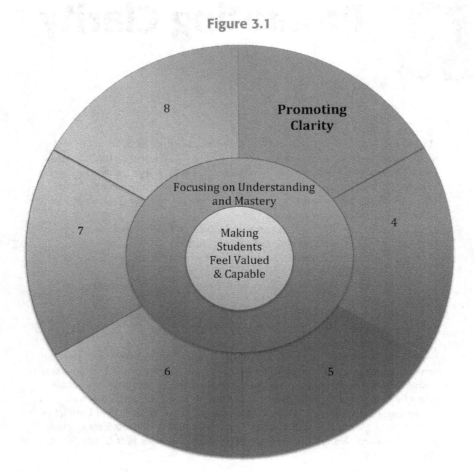

Promoting Clarity in Learning Outcomes

A first step in promoting conceptual understanding is to establish clarity about what students are expected to learn. Effective teachers know specifically what they want to students to master, and they know what they will accept as evidence of mastery. Unlike teachers who might just "cover" the chapter, follow the teacher's guide, or read the script, effective teachers know what they want students to be able to explain, analyze, discuss, solve, perform, or otherwise demonstrate, and they know how well they want students to be able to perform. While these teachers start with the "end in mind," they plan instruction that students are likely to perceive as clear, logical, and understandable.

Hattie (2009) emphasized that teacher clarity had a stronger effect on student achievement than most other variables (almost twice the effect of a typical year of formal schooling). Fisher et al. (2018) described teacher clarity as "the combination of teachers knowing what they are supposed to be teaching, informing students about what they are supposed to be learning, and reaching agreements with students about the success criteria" (p. 15). While these may seem like easy tasks, in many typical urban schools, such clarity has been diminished by strict adherence to teacher manuals or scripts. For example, we have heard teachers answer, "I'm not sure," when asked what they wanted their students to learn from the scripted lesson they had just worked vigorously to follow and teach. On many occasions, we have seen students shrug their shoulders and look lost when we ask, "What are you supposed to be learning in this lesson?" As well, we have observed many lessons where neither the teacher nor the students could tell us how they would know if students had successfully learned the concept being taught.

In our visits to more typical urban schools, we have observed that students often know the topic being covered in the lesson and can sometimes echo the assignment the teacher gave, but they often have limited ideas about what they are expected to know, understand, or be able to do as a result of the lesson. Furthermore, in typical urban schools, we have found very few students who could explain the criteria they could use to know if they succeeded in learning a concept. In response to the question, "How will you know if you have learned the objective well?" we have heard students answer, "I'll know I learned it if I get an 'A' or a 'B' on the test." Fisher et al. (2018) explained that "grades alone serve as poor success criteria" (p. 79).

In response to the same question, we heard a fourth-grade student at Branch Brook School in Newark, New Jersey, explain (as he pointed to the rubric he was using to monitor his progress):

> To earn a five on this assignment, I need to write an opening paragraph that gets the reader's attention. It can't be boring. It's got to make you want to read more. All of the spelling and punctuation have to be perfect, and I've got to use good descriptive words that paint a clear picture for the reader.

In high-performing urban schools, we saw many classrooms where all three of the components described by Fisher et al. were readily apparent. For example, at schools such as Highland Elementary in Silver Springs, Maryland (mentioned at the beginning of this chapter); Horace Mann Elementary School in Glendale, California; R.N. Harris Magnet School in Durham, North Carolina; William Dandy Middle School in Fort Lauderdale, Florida; and Maplewood Richmond Heights High School in St. Louis, Missouri, almost every student could explain what their teacher wanted them to learn, why it was important, and how they would know if they learned it well. Teachers and students shared an understanding of *why* they were engaged in the lesson. There was a clear purpose to the lesson's activities.

Students knew what they were expected to learn, in part, because teachers knew what they wanted their students to understand and master. This clarity about lesson purpose was enhanced through teachers' regular collaboration with colleagues. At almost all of the high-performing urban schools studied, we found that teams of teachers met regularly to specify and discuss what they wanted their students to learn. As a result of their collaboration, teachers could explain the standard they were teaching and discuss how the standard built upon other concepts and built toward other standards to come. Teachers could discuss the level of rigor associated with the standard. Teachers knew, with reasonable specificity, the cognitive tasks their students would be asked to perform and how those tasks differed from easier tasks students were expected to perform at earlier grade levels. Teachers were able to communicate these learning expectations to their students, in part, because the quality of their collaboration efforts helped them understand the learning expectations deeply.

Promoting Clarity in Lesson Organization

Clarity about what students should learn is the foundation of strong lesson design. To effectively build upon the foundation, instruction needs to be organized in a clear and easy-to-follow manner; students should perceive explanations of important ideas as clear, comprehensible, and logical; students should have clear examples to which they can relate; and students should be provided opportunities to participate in guided practice of key concepts and skills. Additionally, there should be assessment strategies that provide useful information about the extent to which students have developed mastery of the learning expectations (Fendick, 1990).

Wiggins and McTighe (2005) contended that teachers increase the likelihood of student understanding by backward mapping: starting with the desired learning outcome and identifying the logical steps that might lead to mastery. This logical approach can lead to strong learning results, even with highly complex academic content.

The goal is not simply for teachers to demonstrate clarity. Teachers make an even more powerful difference when they establish student clarity. "From the perspective of the learner, student clarity is achieved when students know what is to be learned, how they are progressing in their learning, and what they need to learn next" (Almarode & Vandas, 2018, p. 5). Frey, Hattie, and Fisher (2018) referred to students as "assessment-capable" learners when they possessed this type of clarity (p. 1–2). In many of the high-performing urban schools we visited, we observed multiple examples of teachers leading students toward becoming assessment-capable learners.

At Dayton Business and Technology High School, we asked students why they seemed to be learning so much more than they were learning at the schools they attended before they were suspended or expelled. One student explained, "Here, the teachers make it real for us, so what you're learning makes sense. You don't have to read the teacher's mind to figure out what you're supposed to be learning." Then another student asked, "Why couldn't they do that for us at the other school?" And a third responded, "You know 'why.' They [the teachers at the previous schools] didn't care whether we learned or not."

To help ensure that students perceive that lessons "make sense," teachers in high-performing urban schools deliberately plan and deliver instruction to ensure students develop strong understandings of key lesson concepts. In the math lesson at Highland Elementary (described in the chapter opening), the teacher did not rush to present the entire concept of linear equations in one lesson. Instead, he carefully designed a series of lessons that helped students develop an understanding of each of the components. He carefully considered what students needed to understand at each rung of the ladder. Logically and systematically, he moved students from one key concept to the next.

Too often, in more typical lessons, missing rungs render the ladder to understanding impossible for some students to climb. Textbooks and workbooks are often constructed to cover large amounts of material in a minimal number of pages. Sometimes concepts with three, four, or more important components, are presented briefly, absent attention to the important details that might bolster student understanding.

If teachers rely heavily on such teaching tools, their students may experience confusion and frustration.

Cruickshank (1985) emphasized that logical and clear teaching requires planning and effort. He explained that effective teachers have to "orient and prepare students for what is to be taught; communicate content so that students understand; provide illustrations and examples; demonstrate; . . . teach things in a related step-by-step manner; . . . and provide feedback to students about how well they are doing" (1985, p. 44).

The task of dividing learning goals into logical steps may not be necessary when one is teaching simple concepts, requiring a lesser depth of understanding. In contrast, logical and sequential presentations may be essential as teachers focus upon more rigorous standards and learning goals that require substantial utilization of higher-order thinking skills. In high-performing urban schools, we observed teachers tackling rigorous, complex academic standards by identifying a logical sequence of specific objectives students needed to learn in order to master the standard.

Several researchers have referred to the process of breaking complex concepts and skills into a logical sequence of steps as "chunking." Marzano (2007) summarized this research and explained the importance of organizing information into "digestible chunks for students" (p. 34). Nevertheless, when teachers fail to develop a deep understanding of the concepts they are expected to teach, they may have difficulty identifying the important "chunks" into which concepts and skills should be organized. For example, we heard one teacher confess, "When I was in school, I learned how to get the right answer. Nobody asked me why the procedure worked." In contrast, at most of the high-performing schools we studied, teachers had the benefit of working frequently and regularly with colleagues in small groups. They established trusting relationships and were willing to ask each other questions and support each other in deepening their understanding of key concepts and skills.

Teachers must be able to identify the subconcepts and subskills that must be foregrounded and appropriately sequenced if students' are to understand and master more complex concepts and skills. They must be able to predict the associated nuances that might confuse and frustrate students. Through their own mastery of the content (and the pedagogy related to helping students master the content), teachers are better able to plan and deliver a logical sequence of lessons and a logical sequence of activities within a lesson, leading students to deeper levels of understanding.

It is important to note that most principals in high-performing urban schools described regularly scheduled, schoolwide collaboration activities as essential to teachers' developing the content knowledge and the pedagogical skills necessary for organizing clear, powerful, and effective lessons. As teachers challenge one another to define clear learning outcomes, identify factors that might influence students' attainment of the outcomes, and continuously share and examine student work products related to the outcomes, teachers collectively build their own and each other's mastery of content and pedagogy.

While many schools claim to promote teacher collaboration, sometimes less concentrated and consistent efforts fall short of influencing noticeable changes in teaching and learning. In contrast, in many high-performing urban schools like Nueva Vista Elementary in Los Angeles, California, collaboration played a central role in helping teachers develop lessons that were more likely to result in student understanding. Similarly, at Escontrias Elementary in El Paso, Texas (Socorro Independent School District), teachers met in grade-level teams and in vertical teams to discuss the content they intended to teach. In the vertical teams, teachers met with colleagues across grade levels who shared leadership responsibility for specific subject areas (e.g., mathematics or reading). Teachers engaged in detailed conversations about the concepts and skills to be mastered at a given grade level in order to prepared students for the introduction of related concepts and skills at a subsequent grade levels. In grade-level team meetings, teachers discussed what students needed to master in order to meet specific learning expectations. They discussed the specific intricacies of what students needed to know and understand in ways that helped build their own content knowledge. Also, the teachers shared and discussed student work, paying particular attention to the nature of instruction that led some students to deeper levels of understanding.

It is important to note that logically sequenced lessons may take more time to deliver than is often allotted in district pacing guides. As mentioned in Chapter 2, we found principals of high-performing urban schools often encouraged teachers to pursue depth, even if it meant covering fewer topics. To the degree teachers were careful to identify and deliberately teach key concepts in depth, students were more likely to attain mastery of challenging academic standards.

The logical, well-organized introduction of content acknowledges the need for teachers to ensure students understand one concept before they proceed to the next. To the contrary, textbooks and worksheets often push teachers to introduce multiple concepts and then immediately ask students to distinguish the ideas from each other. This sometimes results in a stump-the-students routine whereby teachers pose a question that students have little chance of answering correctly; often the only students who know the answer are those who have mastered the concepts long before the teacher introduced them. Too often, this haphazard routine leads students to make wild guesses that consume time and likely lead to misunderstandings.

Generally, teachers in high-performing urban schools checked meticulously to ensure that students understood one concept before they asked students to distinguish the concept from related concepts and ideas. Teachers worked to ensure that students formed clear mental images of each individual idea, avoiding the confusion that could emerge with introducing too many ideas simultaneously.

Promoting Clarity in the Representation of Ideas

Even if learning purposes are clear to students and students perceive the lesson organization as logical, teachers must still find ways to help students understand each important concept. Teachers use words, images, objects, and interactions to help students develop clear understandings of important ideas. Often, textbooks, worksheets, and other common teaching tools have limited utility in helping many students understand critical ideas, especially when students may have never encountered discussions of the concept at home or when the students' interaction with the concept occurred in a different language or dialect than used at school. Often the words, images, or activities use to convey representations might paint a clearer picture of the concept to one racial/ethnic/cultural group than to another.

Once again, in high-performing schools, teachers benefitted from collaboration with peers as they worked together to consider how to help students conceptualize new ideas. Teachers reported spending considerable time planning with their colleagues in ways that helped their students conceptualize challenging ideas. With their students in mind, teachers planned strategies for building understanding of difficult concepts. For example, at schools like Southside Elementary in Miami, World of Inquiry in Rochester, New York, or Dayton Business and Technology High in Dayton, teachers employed many practical, real-life situations and objects to help students make sense of concepts that students might have perceived as vague or abstract. At schools like Mittie Pullam Elementary in Brownsville, Rose Park Middle School in Nashville, Tennessee; Engineering and Science University Magnet in Hamden, Connecticut; Young Men's Leadership Academy in Fort Worth, Texas, and Keller Dual Immersion Middle School in Long Beach, California, teachers planned project-based learning approaches to help students understand important concepts in mathematics and science.

At schools such as Wesley-Matthews Elementary in Miami and Finney Elementary in Chula Vista, California, clarity was enhanced through the use of thinking maps, graphic organizers, and other nonverbal representations. At these and other schools, we observed teachers using pictures, charts, three-dimensional objects, graphs, concept maps, diagrams, and other tools to help students form a clear understanding of a concept or an idea. For example, at Hambrick Middle School in Houston, Texas, we observed social studies students who used graphic organizers to clarify the differences between the Articles of Confederation and the U.S. Constitution. The graphic organizers helped students articulate key concepts so they were able to write detailed reports that made the distinctions clear to readers. Similarly, we observed fourth-grade students at Bridesburg Elementary in Philadelphia, Pennsylvania, select and use graphic organizers to help them develop expository papers concerning Vietnam. It is as if teachers asked themselves the question, "What can I show my students, say to my students, or have my students do that would make this concept clear to them? In particular, what could I do that would help my students from various racial/ethnic/cultural groups understand this concept?"

Marzano, Pickering, and Pollock (2001) emphasized the value of nonlinguistic representations (visual aids) in promoting clear understandings. They explained that when teachers engage students in creating various kinds of graphic representations, physical models, or pictures, students not only understand the concepts in greater depth but also recall them much more easily.

Just as clarity is facilitated visually, it is also enhanced through auditory means. In high-performing schools, we observed teachers clearly and audibly articulating important ideas. They pronounced words accurately and distinctly, especially when those words were central to the concepts they were teaching. Teachers used vocabulary students understood, at the same time leading students to recall and apply newly introduced vocabulary. Similarly, when teachers engaged students in responding orally (which occurred frequently, as will be described in more detail in Chapter 5), they insisted that students speak audibly and clearly so other students could learn from the conversation. Teachers often encouraged students to pronounce important vocabulary accurately and distinctly.

To enhance clarity, teachers in high-performing urban schools kept presentations of information brief. Rarely did we observe long lectures. Overwhelmingly, we heard student voices more than we heard teacher voices as we visited classrooms.

Often teachers would present a concept in a few minutes and immediately engage students in discussion of the concept or engage students in activity. By keeping the presentation of information brief, teachers forced themselves to be clear and concise. Students knew precisely what they were expected to learn and how they were expected to apply or use the new information.

Rosenshine (2012) found that presenting new material in small steps increased student understanding. When teachers present too much material at once, they may make it difficult or impossible for students to process concepts accurately. Rosenshine explained that more successful teachers did not overwhelm their students by introducing too much at one time; rather, they taught in small steps and then guided their students in practicing the material. In contrast, the least effective teachers presented an entire lesson and then passed out worksheets.

In the urban schools we awarded, many teachers were able to be more concise because they were teaching students strategies for accessing information and finding answers on their own. In other words, these teachers did not present all of the information they wanted students to learn and then hope students would remember all of the lecture's contents. Instead, teachers presented important core ideas and helped students learn how to access information quickly and reliably. For example, the aforementioned teacher of the social studies class at Charles Lunsford Elementary in Rochester, New York, did not offer a lengthy lecture concerning the various facets of life during the Civil War. Instead, she offered a clear explanation of the role she wanted her students to assume as speechwriters for Abraham Lincoln. She explained the importance of the task, and she offered students a cart full of library books from which they could draw general ideas, specific facts, and compelling anecdotes.

By teaching students strategies for acquiring information, teachers can proceed more quickly to challenging academic tasks than they could if they tried to get students to memorize all of the information that is more typically perceived as prerequisite knowledge. For example, in several high-performing elementary schools, teachers reported that they were able to help students progress to more advanced mathematics, even though students had not memorized all of the multiplication facts. Teachers explained that they taught students strategies for getting the correct answer reliably and relatively quickly. A teacher at Signal Hill Elementary in Long Beach, California, explained:

> We could get just about every student to learn to multiply by one, two, three, four, five, and ten. It was harder to get some students to master the rest of the facts. So, we started teaching students how to use the distributive property to make multiplication easy. If they wanted to multiply eight times six, we showed them that it's the same as multiplying eight times five and adding eight times one.

This teacher taught her students a strategy that allowed them to acquire the correct answer reliably. Although students may not have initially demonstrated automaticity with multiplication facts, as many teachers desire, students acquired correct answers and developed a greater sense of personal efficacy concerning mathematics. By consistently acquiring the correct answer, students increased the likelihood of eventual memorization. In the meantime, students were able to advance to more complex mathematical concepts and skills.

Teachers were also able to spend less time presenting information when they helped students learn how to use rubrics or scoring guides to evaluate the quality of their work. Often teachers gave students rubrics before students began working. Sometimes, they engaged students in helping create the scoring rubric. Often, teachers in high-performing schools prompted students to use rubrics as students were completing assignments. This not only resulted in less teacher presentation time but also resulted in students perceiving that they could ensure their own academic success.

Summary

Popham (2008) suggested a four-step strategy for building lessons that promoted understanding. The four steps included "(1) thoroughly understanding the target curriculum aim, (2) identifying all requisite precursory sub-skills and bodies of enabling knowledge, (3) determining whether students' status with respect to each preliminarily identified building block can be measured, and (4) arranging all building blocks in an instructionally defensible sequence" (2008, p. 47). In our study of high-performing urban schools, we have observed similar practices as teachers endeavored to promote clarity.

In high-performing urban schools, teachers promoted clarity by first making clear to themselves what they wanted their students to know and understand, by making learning expectations clear to students, and by helping students understand the criteria by which learning success should be assessed. Additionally, teachers promoted clarity by developing lessons that were organized in ways that made the content seem logical and coherent. As well, teachers advanced clarity by presenting concepts in ways that their students (including all of their various racial/ethnic/cultural groups of students) were likely to understand. Through the use of activities (e.g., project-based learning), visual cues (e.g., graphic organizers, pictures, objects, thinking maps), and clear and concise auditory messages (e.g., brief lectures highlighting enumerated points), teachers helped students develop accurate conceptualizations of challenging concepts. Teacher collaboration played a major role in helping teachers develop the teaching strategies and approaches needed to promote clarity. To maximize clarity for every student, teachers in high-performing urban schools taught in ways that were culturally, socially, and personally responsive. This practice is described in greater detail in Chapter 4.

Ultimately, clarity is in the mind of the beholder. What is clear to the teacher may not be clear to each student. By asking students to restate key concepts and ideas, many teachers made certain that students clearly understood important concepts. Even when teachers had worked together to plan detailed, carefully sequenced, clear lessons, they checked to make sure that students could use their own words to describe or explain the major concepts teachers wanted their students to learn. This practice of checking for understanding is also described in greater detail in Chapter 5.

What It Is & What It Isn't

Promoting Clarity

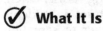 What It Is

Helping students develop a clear understanding of what they are expected to learn as a result of a lesson

> Example: When the teacher asked her third-grade students to describe planets, students answered by citing planet names (e.g., Mercury, Venus, Earth, Jupiter, Saturn). When the teacher asked students how planets were different from stars, it became clear quickly that students could not articulate the distinction. Then, the teacher explained that, by the end of the lesson, students would be able to define planets, define stars, and describe the ways in which planets and stars differ. Also, the teacher explained that students needed to be able to describe at least one way in which planets and stars were similar. Then, the teacher led the students in a discussion about why it might be useful to know the differences between planets and stars. The teacher asked students to work in groups to develop lists of questions they should be able to answer at the end of the lesson. The teacher explained that their questions had to address (1) the characteristics of planets, (2) the characteristics of stars, (3) the differences between planets and stars, or (4) the similarities between planets and stars. The whole class discussed the questions the groups developed, and the teacher affirmed which questions students should be able to answer by the lesson's end.

⊗ What It Isn't

Engaging students in a lesson without ever giving students a clear sense of what they are expected to learn.

> Example: The teacher organized the class into small groups. Each group was expected to read a chapter in the science book concerning stars and planets. As groups finished reading, the teacher asked students to work together to answer the questions at the end of the chapter. Students followed the directions, but they did not know what they were expected to know or understand as a result of reading the chapter.

⊘ What It Is

Breaking down complex tasks or concepts into a logical progression or sequence that students are likely to see as rationale.

> Example: The history teacher wanted students to understand that human needs and desires influence political decisions (including

some decisions that might seem counterproductive). First, the teacher engaged students in reading and discussing articles that described how people in Germany admired Hitler in the late 1930s. Then the teacher asked groups of students to discuss why German citizens chose to follow Hitler. Student comments suggested that the German people were hateful, bigoted, evil, or crazy. Next, the teacher led students to review and discuss a series of articles about the sanctions the Allies placed on Germany at the end of World War I and the economic impact of those sanctions. Then the teacher engaged the students in discussions about the impact of the Great Depression on Germany and the lives of the German people. Finally, the teacher invited student groups to reconsider the reasons the German people admired Hitler in the late 1930s. Students recognized that many German citizens saw Hitler as someone who would help them regain economic strength, reduce poverty, and restore Germany as a respected world power. While the students still understood the evils of the Nazi regime, the students understood how ordinary human needs and desires influenced the German citizens' willingness to accept Hitler as a leader.

(X) What It Isn't

Teaching complex concepts without identifying, distinguishing, or sequencing the elements or the steps involved in understanding

Example: The history teacher presented a chapter on the causes of World War II as one lesson with a huge mix of facts, dates, personalities, and contexts. Students completed the lesson without understanding why the German people chose to follow Adolph Hitler.

(✓) What It Is

Making sure students attain clarity regarding one concept before advancing to the next related concept

Example: The music teacher defined quarter notes, modeled examples of playing quarter notes, and gave students multiple opportunities to play quarter notes. When the teacher was fairly certain that students understood quarter notes, he introduced the concept of triplets.

(X) What It Isn't

Trying to get students to differentiate related ideas before they have clarity about any of the ideas being taught

Example: The teacher played four measures of quarter notes, then played four measures of half notes, and then played four measures of triplets. Immediately, the teacher asked students to distinguish between the three types of notes. While some students answered correctly, many students made random guesses because they did not understand the distinctions. Some students might have confused the number of measures played with the number of beats within a measure.

✓ What It Is

Enhancing clarity through visual representations

Example: The teacher helped students create Venn diagrams that illustrate the similarities and differences of plant and animal cells. Then students used their diagrams as visual aids as they reported their findings to peers.

✗ What It Isn't

Expecting students to understand simply by reading text or listening to a lecture

Example: Students read a chapter about plant and animal cell characteristics and then answered the questions at the chapter's end.

✓ What It Is

Checking to ensure that content, directions, and concepts are perceived clearly by all students

Example: The teacher asked students to write a letter to a friend that explained the steps the friend should use when he or she attempted to identify a pattern in a sequence of numbers. While students were writing, the teacher checked to ensure that students were explaining the steps accurately and clearly.

✗ What It Isn't

Assuming that students perceive what is presented clearly

Example: The teacher listed the steps students should use when they attempted to identify a pattern in a sequence of numbers. Then the teacher asked, "Any questions?" After waiting five seconds, the teacher covered the list of steps and then asked students to recreate the list individually. Then the teacher went to his desk to grade homework papers.

✓ What It Is

Anticipating possible misconceptions and teaching to prevent them

Example: As the elementary teachers planned how they would teach the concept of area of polygons, they recognized the possibility that students would confuse area with perimeter. They designed a set of experiences that would first engage students in studying the etymology of the term *perimeter*. Next, they planned to engage students in identifying, practicing, and discussing common uses of the term *area*. In particular, they planned to have students try to describe the size of a space without using square measurements. Finally, they engaged students in choosing to use *perimeter tools* (rulers, yarn, yardsticks, and popsicle sticks) or *area tools* (one-centimeter square tiles, one-inch square tiles, and one-foot square tiles) to measure a variety of objects in the classroom. They planned to require students to articulate their rationale for their choice of measurement tools.

⊗ What It Isn't

Presenting without considering possible student misconceptions

> Example: The teachers planned to introduce the concept of perimeter on Monday and require students to answer the items on page 25 of the workbook. Then they planned to introduce the concept of area on Tuesday and require students to answer the items on page 26.

⊘ What It Is

Keeping presentations of information brief

> Example: The teacher presented short two-minute clips from a movie. Each clip included examples of characters using figurative language. After each clip, the teacher engaged students in a discussion of the examples and types of figurative language observed.

⊗ What It Isn't

Long presentations

> Example: The teacher presented a feature-length film with many great examples of characters using figurative language. At the conclusion of the film, the teacher asked students to recall some of the examples of figurative language used in the film.

⊘ What It Is

Teaching students strategies

> Example: After a set of activities in which students discussed examples of personification, the teacher explained to students that they could identify an example of an author's use of personification through a two-step process. First, the teacher asked students to identify text in which the author mentioned a nonhuman object. Second, students were asked to determine if the author described the nonhuman object in a way that would typically be used to

describe a person. Using this two-step process, pairs of students worked together to identify examples of personification. Then students were asked to explain why the words they identified represented examples of personification.

(X) What It Isn't

Expecting students to "figure it out"

> Example: The teacher explained what personification means, high-lighted some examples of personification, and then asked students to identify and copy examples of personification found in a poem.

(✓) What It Is

Teaching students how to access information

> Example: The teacher helped students identify key words they could use on a variety of search engines to access information about the Lincoln-Douglas debates. Students then used the search engines to acquire information and organize a report of major themes and arguments from the debates.

(X) What It Isn't

Expecting students to memorize information

> Example: The teacher presents a lecture about the Lincoln-Douglas debates. Students were expected to take notes and remember major themes and arguments from the debates.

Practice Guide Related to Promoting Clarity

For information on possible uses of this practice guide, please see page xiii in the Preface.

Table 3.1

1. Did students understand specifically what they were being asked to learn? Did students understand what success criteria would be used to assess their understanding of the learning goal?	(Y)	(N)
2. Did the teacher break down complex ideas, concepts, or tasks into logical steps and teach one at a time?	(Y)	(N)
3. Did the teacher anticipate possible misunderstandings and teach accordingly?	(Y)	(N)
4. Did students understand/follow the presentation of information?	(Y)	(N)
5. Did the teacher ensure student mastery of one concept before presenting a second one?	(Y)	(N)
6. Could all students hear the instruction well?	(Y)	(N)

7. Did students restate important rules, procedures, or concepts?	Ⓨ	Ⓝ
8. Did the teacher use nonverbal representations in order to make the information clearer to students?	Ⓨ	Ⓝ
9. Did all students provide evidence that they understood the concepts being presented?	Ⓨ	Ⓝ
10. Did the teacher keep the presentation of new information brief?	Ⓨ	Ⓝ
11. Did the teacher present complex ideas in "chunks" and provide time for students to demonstrate understanding of one piece before proceeding to the next?	Ⓨ	Ⓝ
12. Did students learn strategies for acquiring key concepts (minimizing reliance on memory)?	Ⓨ	Ⓝ
13. Did the teacher give students rubrics so they could evaluate the quality of their work?	Ⓨ	Ⓝ

In a strong lesson, a "yes" answer is recorded for at least seven of these items.
In an outstanding lesson, a "yes" answer is recorded for at least ten of these items.

Practical Next Steps

1. In collaboration with teacher colleagues, engage in a book study of *The Skillful Teacher: Building Your Teaching Skills* (Saphier et al., 2008). In particular, read Chapter 9 that explores a variety of strategies teachers can use to promote the clear and logical presentation of information. Choose strategies that you will endeavor to implement in your classroom. Invite a colleague to observe and comment about the ways in which you are implementing the strategy well and ways in which you might improve implementation. Provide similar observation and feedback for a colleague.

2. Invite a colleague to observe your classroom. (Select a colleague who has not worked with you to plan lessons.) Ask the colleague to write down what they believe you want your students to understand by the end of the lesson. Also, ask them to write down what they believe are the success criteria you will use to assess whether students have mastered the concept or skill. Then ask the colleague to randomly ask students what they believe you want them to learn as a result of the lesson. Also, ask the colleague to ask students about the criteria you will use to assess student success. Invite the colleagues to share their findings. And offer to provide the same observation and feedback in support of your colleague.

3. With the colleagues in your grade-level team or subject-area team, select a learning objective that students did not master well. Together, plan a set of strategies for (a) making the learning outcomes and success criteria clear to students, (b) organizing lessons in a way that will have a higher likelihood of resonating with your students and advancing their understanding, and (c) presenting key concepts through projects, visual representations, or auditory means

that are more likely to generate deep understanding among your students. After implementing the lessons, examine student work together using the success criteria you developed. Determine what practices might have been useful in advancing understanding. Determine what practices might be improved to generate higher levels of understanding.

References

Almarode, J., & Vandas, K. (2018). *Clarity for learning: Five essential practices that empower students and teachers.* Thousand Oaks, CA: Corwin.

Cruickshank, D. R. (1985). Applying research on teacher clarity. *Journal of Teacher Education, 35*(4), 44–48.

Fendick, F. (1990). *Correlation between teacher clarity of communication and student achievement gain: A meta-analysis* (Doctoral dissertation). Retrieved from Pro-Quest Dissertation Express. (UMI No. 9115979).

Fisher, D., Frey, N., Quaglia, R. J., Smith, D., & Lande, L. L. (2018). *Engagement by design: Creating learning environments where students thrive.* Thousand Oaks, CA: Corwin.

Frey, N., Hattie, J., & Fisher, D. (2018). *Developing assessment-capable visible learners grades K-12: Maximizing skill, will, and thrill.* Thousand Oaks, CA: Corwin.

Hattie, J. A. C. (2009). *Visible learning: A synthesis of over 800 meta-analyses relating to achievement.* Abingdon, Oxon: Routledge.

Marzano, R. J. (2007). *The art and science of teaching: A comprehensive framework for effective instruction.* Alexandria, VA: Association for Supervision and Curriculum Development.

Marzano, R. J., Pickering, D. J., & Pollock, J. E. (2001). *Classroom instruction that works: Research-based strategies for increasing student achievement.* Alexandria, VA: Association for Supervision and Curriculum Development.

Popham, W. J. (2008). *Transformative assessment.* Alexandria, VA: Association for Supervision and Curriculum Development.

Rosenshine, B. (2012, Spring). Principles of instruction: Research-based strategies that all teachers should know. *American Educator*, 12–39.

Saphier, J., Haley-Speca, M. A., & Gower, R. (2008). *The skillful teacher: Building your teaching skills.* Acton, MA: Research for Better Teaching.

Wiggins, G. P., & McTighe, J. (2005). *Understanding by design* (Expanded 2nd ed.). Upper Saddle River, NJ: Pearson Education, Inc.

4 Ensuring Culturally, Socially, and Personally Responsive Teaching

As usual, the conversations in this sophomore English class at Lawndale High School near Los Angeles, California, were intense. Groups of three or four students (mostly Latino and African American) were leaning in, talking to each other with an air of urgency. Everyone was on task. The teacher floated from group to group, offering suggestions, but the students clearly were self-directed. Each group had the task of rewriting a scene from Shakespeare's King Lear. *The students had to rewrite their scene in a manner that would be easily and completely understood by any of their peers. Students were using their notes from the prior class conversation, as well as the well-worn pages of the play, to help them confer, discuss, and even argue about the appropriate language that would best communicate the scene's meaning to their peers.*

A student in one group read from Act 4, Scene 1, "As flies to wanton boys are we to the gods. They kill us for their sport."

Instantly, another explained, "The dude is bummed out. They blinded him." "Yeah, but how should we rewrite his line?" prompted another student. "Kids aren't going to get what 'flies to wanton boys' means."

The student who had read the line offered a suggestion. "How about if we rewrite it to say, 'Life is messed up!'"

"That's good," one of the students offered, "but he needs to say something about how he's blaming the gods."

After thinking for a minute, a student suggested, "Life is messed up! The gods are just playin' us!"

The others nodded in agreement. They wrote the line and went to another paragraph in the play where students anticipated the need for making the language more accessible to their peers.

One student told his classmates, "You can't leave the word 'sepulcher' in there. Kids aren't going to know that word. How about 'crypt'? They've seen scary movies. They'll know what that means."

Lawndale High School is in the Centinela Valley Union High School District near Los Angeles, California. The school serves approximately 1,550 students in grades nine through twelve. The school won the America's Best Urban Schools Award in 2009.

A Perpetual Question

On the Minds of Educators Striving to Produce Equity and Excellence

How can I get each and every one of my students to think, "Oh! I get this! I know about this! This makes sense to me and my life"?

Teachers in high-performing urban schools help more students achieve understanding and mastery, at least in part, because they teach concepts in ways that resonate with their students. Often in collaboration with their colleagues, teachers ask themselves, "How can I get *my* students to understand this challenging concept?" "How can I get *my* students to see this as familiar?" "How can I get *my* students to see the connection between their interests, backgrounds, cultures, and prior knowledge and this important academic idea?" As a result, teachers are more likely to produce lessons that connect with the interests, backgrounds, cultures, and prior knowledge of their students.

In high-performing urban schools, we observed many examples of culturally responsive teaching. Hammond (2015) defined culturally responsive teaching as:

> . . . an educator's ability to recognize students' cultural displays of learning and meaning making and respond positively and constructively with teaching moves that use cultural knowledge as a scaffold to connect what the student knows to new concepts and content in order to promote effective **information processing**. All the while, the educator understands the importance of being in a relationship and having a social-emotional connection to the student in order to create a safe place for learning.
>
> (p. 15)

In many successful elementary, middle, and high schools, we saw examples of teachers using their cultural knowledge of their students "as a scaffold to connect" their students' knowledge, background, and experiences with the challenging content they wanted all their students to learn. Similarly, we observed teachers using their knowledge of students' personal and social situations to achieve the same goal. Thus, we label the practice we observed as "culturally, socially, and personally responsive teaching." Some scholars might argue that the social and personal aspects are simply components of cultural knowledge. To ensure that readers acknowledge the importance of responding to and building upon students' social and personal knowledge, background, and interests, we have chosen to draw distinct attention to these concerns.

As suggested in Figure 4.1, and as highlighted in Hammond's definition, through culturally, socially, and personally responsive teaching, educators deepen their students' clarity about important concepts. As well, they enhance the focus on understanding and mastery and reinforce powerful messages about the extent to which their students are valued and capable.

Assuming Student Ability

Teachers at the schools we studied evidenced a strong belief that their students could learn challenging concepts. While teachers at other schools, serving low-income students of color, worried that it might be impossible to get their students to master more rigorous state standards, teachers in the high-performing urban

Figure 4.1

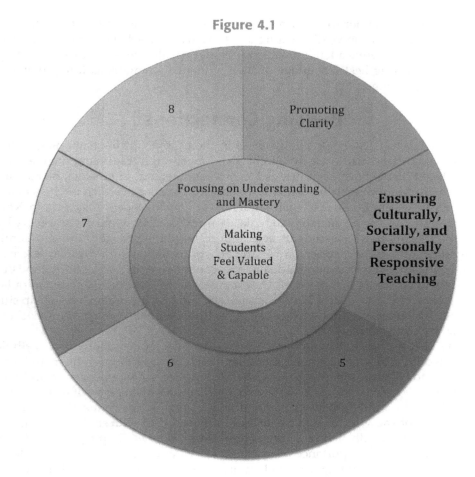

schools tended to assume that their students could and would excel. Across the various schools we studied, we heard many teachers echo the sentiment of a teacher at Escontrias Elementary in El Paso, Texas, who explained, "We know they [our students] can achieve anything. We just have to find a way to get them to learn it."

The assumption that students can achieve at high levels is essential because, in its absence, there is no reason to struggle to find the strategies that will lead diverse students to academic excellence. It is difficult to imagine teachers working diligently to find more effective ways to teach a skill if they assume their students are incapable of learning and destined to fail. Unfortunately, some teachers may perceive that they have conclusive evidence that their students are unlikely to succeed at learning rigorous content. Sometimes, these teachers possess multiple years of experience observing their students fail. Apart from placating their administrators, they see no reason to try different instructional approaches because they already know the outcome will be failure and frustration.

In contrast, educators in high-performing urban schools have learned to share effective lesson strategies tailored to the strengths, interests, and backgrounds of their students. One teacher's success in ensuring that students master a concept in biology leads another to apply a similar strategy in the teaching of a chemistry principle. Successes snowball, creating a culture where teachers assume that their students can achieve academic excellence if they create the appropriate learning opportunity, taking best advantage of their students' strengths, culture, interests, and prior knowledge.

Building Connections

The teacher at Lawndale High School in the example at the beginning of the chapter could have just as easily taught Shakespeare in a traditional manner, but would his students have been just as likely to understand, internalize, or remember? In high-performing urban schools, we observed lessons in which teachers made new concepts seem familiar to their students. At Dreamkeepers Academy in Norfolk, Virginia, we saw elementary students learn and practice Spanish vocabulary by performing skits in which students acted out restaurant scenes and ordered familiar foods. Similarly, at Henderson Middle School in Richmond, Virginia, teachers employed a variety of visual, hands-on, and cooperative instructional methods to make sure their students succeeded. They regularly used learning games, manipulatives, technology, flow charts, hands-on projects, and graphic organizers to help students connect their prior knowledge and experiences with the content their teachers were endeavoring to teach.

Gay (2010) argued that underachieving students from various racial/ethnic groups would achieve much more if teachers taught to and through their students' personal and cultural strengths, prior accomplishments, and experiences. In the high-performing schools we studied, we saw many examples of this type of instruction.

Perhaps it should go without saying that it is difficult to "connect" with someone you do not know. In order to create lessons that connect with students culturally, socially, and personally, teachers must know their students. Delpit (2005) and Gay (2010) described the importance of teachers' knowing the cultures of the students they serve so that they might provide more effective instruction. As discussed in Chapter 1, many teachers in high-performing urban schools made deliberate efforts to learn about their students and their students' families. By learning about their students' traditions, values, language patterns, interests, pastimes, routines, and aspirations, teachers learned what their students were most eager to read, what their students loved to eat, what their students would stay up late to play on their technological devices or watch on television. Teachers learned what piqued the interest of their students and they developed, designed, or modified lessons accordingly.

Often, the development of lessons occurred in team collaboration meetings. In these meetings, teachers came to realize that some of their existing textbooks and other curricular materials were not likely to resonate with their students. They recognized that it might be difficult to lead their students to deep understandings of certain concepts if the only teaching tools at their disposal were designed for White, middle-class students who had a vastly different set of life experiences and interests.

Teachers shared that their efforts to develop intriguing, powerful lessons took time and energy. Teachers shared that they worked in collaboration with their peers to build lessons that would create "aha" experiences in which students made sense of new concepts by connecting the new ideas to situations they had experienced or interests that excited them. Often, teachers used collaboration times (e.g., department meetings, grade-level planning meetings, professional learning communities) to pool their best ideas and generate lessons that students would perceive as interesting, relevant, or even fun. Working collaboratively, teachers searched for, developed, adapted, or stumbled upon teaching strategies and materials that offered greater promise of connecting with their students. In some cases, teachers determined that new materials weren't needed if they were creative about how they used existing materials. In some cases, teachers discovered that an approach one teacher developed and tried might be adapted and used by others on the team. In other cases, teachers worked together to develop new lessons that were more likely to be culturally, socially, and personally responsive to their students.

Ensuring Culturally Responsive Teaching

Culture matters. Hammond (2015) explained, "Culture, it turns out, is the way that every brain makes sense of the world. . . . The brain uses cultural information to turn everyday happenings into meaningful events" (p. 22). Lessons are never culturally neutral. Lessons can be structured in ways that make it easier or more difficult for students to make sense of concepts.

Similarly, Ginsberg and Wlodkowski (2000) explained, "Because the socialization of emotions is influenced by cultural experiences, the motivational response a student has to a learning activity reflects this influence and its associated complexity" (p. 43). A lesson might spark a powerful motivational response in some students and leave other students yawning. This is a particular challenge when educators are endeavoring to make a positive difference for students from diverse racial, ethnic, socio-economic, and linguistic backgrounds. Similarly, it is a challenge for educators who were taught teaching strategies and/or provided teaching materials designed to respond to the learning strengths of a cultural group different from the students they currently have the privilege to serve.

In contrast, researchers have determined that teachers who utilize culturally responsive teaching practices are more likely to help their students succeed academically. For example, Howard (2001) and Ladson-Billings (2009) examined the pedagogical practices of highly effective elementary teachers who taught African American students in urban settings. The teachers consistently used culturally responsive pedagogy, designing lessons featuring challenging academic concepts in ways that were relevant to, sensitive to, and responsive to the cultural differences of students.

Gay (2010) described four aspects of culturally responsive teaching: caring, communication, curriculum, and instruction. Caring was discussed explicitly in Chapter 1. In high-performing urban schools, educators made impressive efforts to ensure that all students across the various cultural groups served perceived they were both valued and capable. Communication was discussed in Chapter 3. Teachers in high-performing urban schools used auditory and visual strategies, along with various active engagement strategies, to communicate concepts in ways that made sense to all the students they served.

In high-performing urban schools, we also observed teachers strategically enhancing the curriculum and their instructional practice to advance culturally responsive teaching. While teachers did not lose sight of the learning goals associated with the standards they wanted their students to master, they often broadened the prescribed curriculum by adding elements that would have greater relevance and interest for their students. For example, a discussion about the European imperialistic practices in Africa in the early twentieth century generated powerful student interest among students at Lawndale High School and helped students better understand the learning objective focused on the economic forces influencing policies and practices during the industrial age.

Similarly, a discussion about immigration policy today stirred great involvement in a lesson at Veterans Memorial Early College High School in Brownsville, Texas. The history lesson focused on the importance of various battle outcomes in Texas's fight for independence. By broadening the traditional approach to teaching the objective with a discussion of current immigration policy, the teacher engaged students in a manner that led them into deeper discussions of facts, issues, and perspectives.

In addition to broadening the curriculum (what students learned), teachers in many high-performing schools also modified instructional approaches (how students learned) in a way that was culturally responsive to their students. For example, at schools like Wildflower Elementary in Colorado Springs, Colorado, teachers are expected to differentiate instruction in ways that lead diverse groups of students to deeper understanding. Teachers at Wildflower utilize their version of an *Understanding by Design* (Wiggins & McTighe, 2005) planning process to help ensure that lessons will build upon the cultural and linguistic strengths of their students. Similarly, teachers at Oakshire Elementary School in Orlando, Florida, meet in collaborative teams to plan differentiated lessons designed to help all of the school's students master challenging academic standards.

In a large number of high-performing schools, we observed teachers translating a word into Spanish or providing a brief explanation in Spanish when it was clear that students needed more assistance in order to understand a concept. The teachers enhanced the likelihood that their students with emerging bilingualism understood the concepts they wanted students to learn.

In other high-performing urban schools, teachers modified instruction in ways that capitalized even more on the strengths their students had developed in their first language. For example, in schools such as Excellence and Justice in Education Academy in San Diego, California; Horace Mann Dual Language Magnet in Wichita, Kansas; El Sol Science and Arts Academy in Santa Ana, California; Keller Dual Immersion Middle School in Long Beach, California; Nestor Language Academy in San Diego, California; and World Languages Institute in Fort Worth, Texas, students received instruction that accelerated their learning of academic concepts through their native language at the same time they developed fluency and academic skill in a second or even a third language.

In their studies of high-performing schools, Reyes, Scribner, and Scribner (1999) determined that the educators they observed valued students' first language and their home culture. As well, the authors reported that teachers in schools where diverse language learners excelled tailored lessons in ways that connected to the backgrounds, cultures, and experiences of the students they served. Although specific language instruction strategies differed, teachers in high-performing schools treated their students' native language strengths as assets to be valued and utilized in ways that might advance students' understanding of important concepts and skills.

We observed teachers adapting instructional approaches to improve student learning in various subjects, including those that some might think of as culturally neutral, such as mathematics. Germain-McCarthy and Owens (2005) emphasized that mathematics instruction can be enhanced through culturally responsive teaching. They explained:

> Many students today perceive mathematics to be a bunch of numbers that plug into formulas to solve problems. More often than not, the problems they are asked to solve are not their problems, nor do they come close to something they are interested in pursuing.

(p. 5)

In contrast, Germain-McCarthy and Owens offered many suggestions describing how teachers can make mathematics come to life for students from different cultural backgrounds. In the high-performing schools we studied, we observed teachers modifying the word problems in textbooks and workbooks to better resonate with the cultural backgrounds of their students. Teachers seemed to recognize that most of the textbook authors had never met their students, lived in their neighborhoods, or understood their languages or dialects.

Gay (2010) noted that many students of color are more likely to respond to instructional strategies that promote active engagement. While individual students differ and no strategy works for every student, Gay noted that many students of color are less likely to achieve deep levels of understanding with teaching strategies that require students to sit passively and listen. Accordingly, we have observed many classrooms in high-performing urban schools where students are engaged in performing, discussing, creating, building, or similarly active experiences that lead them to deeper understanding of challenging concepts and skills. At high schools like Eastlake High in El Paso, Texas, or Kearny School of International Business in San Diego, California; at middle schools like Keller Dual Immersion Middle School in Long Beach or Hialeah Gardens Middle School in Miami, Florida; or at elementary schools like Fay Herron Elementary School in Las Vegas, Wasena Elementary in Roanoke, Virginia, or at George Washington Elementary in Chicago, Illinois, active student engagement is commonplace.

It is important to note that in high-performing schools, lessons are rarely designed or pursued simply because they are likely to actively engage students. In contrast, teachers are keenly focused on getting students to master key academic concepts and skills. Almost always, these concepts and skills are rooted in state and district standards. Teachers approach the teaching of these concepts and skills in ways that stimulate active student engagement.

The first priority is teaching the content students must learn in order to succeed academically and in life. A second and essential consideration is how teachers might deliver the content in ways that resonate with their students and promote deep understanding. In other words, teachers in high-performing urban schools are not likely to teach a unit on hip-hop music just because it might get students out of their seats. They would, however, be more likely to use hip-hop music to teach a state standard that focused on the use of rhyme and meter in poetry.

Ensuring Socially and Personally Responsive Teaching

We do not wish to imply that social issues or personal issues are distinct from cultural issues. Instead, we want to acknowledge that we observed many educators at high-performing urban schools who provided lessons that tapped into students' social and personal interests. These lessons were not necessarily focused on issues of race, ethnicity, or language but addressed social and personal concerns that were important to students. As well, we observed lessons in which teachers increased student engagement by utilizing popular media (television shows, movies, music, cartoons, plays, etc.), technology (mobile devices, websites, apps, etc.), or other popular activities (sports, games, pastimes). By teaching in ways that responded to students' social or personal interests and concerns, teachers were able to generate better student attendance, greater student engagement, and better learning results.

At several schools (e.g., R.N. Harris Integrated Arts in Durham, North Carolina; Muller Elementary in Tampa, Florida; Hambrick Middle School in Houston, Texas; and Cecil Parker Elementary in Mount Vernon, New York), we saw innovative uses of art, music, dance, physical education, and drama to reinforce important academic concepts related to mathematics, reading, science, writing, and social studies. Teachers cleverly tapped into student interests and backgrounds in ways that helped students relate to and understand important academic concepts. Teachers used art to help students learn geometric concepts related to symmetry, rotation, and parallelism. They used sheet music to reinforce concepts and skills related to fractions. They used games played during physical education to help students practice multiplication facts.

While it is important to note that not every lesson was innovative or inspiring, at the high-performing schools we visited, we saw many examples of teachers presenting challenging academic content in ways that helped students relate the concepts and skills to their prior knowledge, interests, backgrounds, and cultures. For example, at Revere High School in Boston, Massachusetts, a teacher used the popular television show *The Walking Dead* to teach plot points, character development, persuasive writing, and other important concepts and skills (Chiles, 2018).

At Pace Early College High School in Brownsville, Texas, a teacher used clips from the television show *Grey's Anatomy* to help students understand and distinguish the difference between soliloquys, monologues, dialogue, and asides. After students developed an understanding of these terms, the students applied the concepts as they read Shakespeare's *Romeo and Juliet*.

A math teacher at Franklin Towne Charter High in Philadelphia, Pennsylvania, explained, "If I just have them [my students] do what's in the textbook, they probably won't understand. I've got to figure out how to make it come to life for them. Somehow, I've got to make it real to them." Many teachers in the high-performing urban schools we studied evidenced a similar commitment.

Teachers at El Sol Science and Arts Academy in Santa Ana, California, engaged their students in using their bilingual skills in service projects. For example, the students translated menus for local restaurants and for nurse practitioners at community health fairs.

Teachers knew what excited their students, what prompted quiet students to talk, and what motivated students to keep working after the class period ended. They used this knowledge as leverage to help students develop deep understandings of important concepts and skills. As well, teachers used their knowledge of students in a way that strengthened relationships and helped students know they were both valued and capable.

Summary

At high-performing urban schools, teachers begin with the assumption that all of their students can learn challenging academic concepts if they find ways to present information that respond to their students' cultural, social, and personal strengths, interests, and needs. Working with their colleagues, teachers strive to prepare lessons that will build connections between their students and the standards they want their students to learn.

We observed teachers in high-performing urban schools developing and teaching lessons designed to respond to their students' cultural backgrounds. In addition to broadening the curriculum (what is taught) to encompass information students would perceive as culturally relevant, teachers also adapted instruction (how they taught) so that they better responded to the cultural strengths and interests of their students.

Additionally, we found many teachers in high-performing urban schools who advanced student learning by responding to the social and personal needs of their students. Teachers utilized popular media, technological tools, and popular events to pique student interest and advance student understanding of complex ideas.

In most classrooms, planning culturally, socially, and personally responsive lessons meant differentiating instruction. Tomlinson (1999) explained:

> Teachers in differentiated classrooms begin with a clear and solid sense of what constitutes powerful curriculum and engaging instruction. Then they ask what it will take to modify that instruction so that each learner comes away with understandings and skills that offer guidance to the next phase of learning. Essentially, teachers in differentiated classrooms accept, embrace, and plan for the fact that learners bring many commonalities to school, but that learners also bring the essential differences that make them individuals.
>
> (p. 2)

A teacher at William Dandy Middle School in Fort Lauderdale, Florida, explained that generating interesting, engaging lessons is not easy. "Sometimes, we think that we've come up with a lesson that students will relate to. We'll try it out and we'll see that students really aren't getting it. So, we sometimes have to stop in the middle of a lesson and switch it up."

Even when teachers believe they have planned lessons that will connect with their students' interests, backgrounds, cultures, and prior knowledge, they observe closely to determine if students understand key concepts and ideas. If students do not understand, teachers modify their approaches and use different examples and activities that are more likely to make the content come to life for students. As teachers observe and find students struggling, they build in additional examples, aids, steps, or supports to help increase student mastery. Often these supports are ideas that better connect to students' backgrounds, interests, and prior knowledge.

At the same time, as teachers observe and find students excelling, they build in opportunities to extend concepts and deepen understanding. For example, at Horace Mann Elementary and Columbus Elementary in Glendale, California, teachers gave "must do" and "may do" assignments. The "may do" assignments extended upon essentials and provided students greater opportunities to apply what learned to real situations. At the World of Inquiry School in Rochester, New York, students engaged in exciting projects that allowed them to see how the core academic concepts they learned are connected to their experiences. At Mueller Charter School in Chula Vista, California, students used the local nature center as their laboratory, learning about ecological issues that influence their community. Teachers do not assume they have succeeded in advancing the learning of their students just because they designed a lesson intended to respond to the cultural, social, and personal needs of their students. They check to ensure that learning occurred, they provide rich, useful, and specific feedback, and they adapt their next instruction accordingly. The practice of checking understanding and providing feedback will be discussed further in Chapter 5.

What It Is & What It Isn't

Culturally, Socially, and Personally Responsive Teaching

✓ What It Is

Planning lessons that will teach important academic objectives by including activities, examples, or resources to which students are likely to relate

> Example: A biology teacher engages students in a discussion of people they have encountered who have various genetic disorders. They talk about the prevalence rate of each type of disorder for the general population and for specific racial/ethnic groups in the population. Then the teacher assigns various small groups of students the task of finding the genetic source of a specific disorder. Students must create presentations that explain the genetic cause of the disorder and illustrate the genetic dysfunction. They must explain how one might predict the likelihood that various pairs of parents would have a child with the disorder.

✗ What It Isn't

Assuming students will relate to and understand abstract presentations of information

> Example: A biology teacher has students read Chapter 4 of the biology book, which focuses on genetics. After students read the chapter, the teacher provides a lecture that reiterates the major concepts presented in the chapter.

✓ What It Is

Getting to know one's students

> Example: A middle school teacher stands at the classroom door and greets students as they come into his science class. Before he asks one student to remove the headphones from his ears, he asks the student what song is playing. Quietly, he asks another student how his evening went. Then, as students are sitting down, he asks, "Who likes their music loud?" When almost all of the students roar affirmatively, he asks, "How loud is loud? How do you know how loud you like it?" Students can't figure out how to respond. Then the teacher explains that by the end of the class period, the students will know how to measure volume and pitch and assess risks to hearing.

✗ What It Isn't

Not taking time to get to know one's students

Example: The middle school science teacher asks a student to remove his headphones and reminds the student of the rules. The teacher then presents a lesson on sound volume and frequency by covering a worksheet that displays the typical decibel range of various types of noises and the sound frequency range of various symphonic instruments.

⊘ What It Is

Pursuing interesting or fun lessons because they relate to important academic objectives

Example: A teacher is trying to help students practice the challenging vocabulary they are learning in economics. The teacher engages students in creating a question/answer format, similar to a television game show that is wildly popular with teenagers. However, all of the questions are designed to assess students' knowledge of the economics vocabulary learned over the past several weeks. After the questions/answers are developed, the students divide into teams and play the game using the questions/answers they created.

⊗ What It Isn't

Pursuing interesting or fun lessons that will not help students learn important academic objectives

Example: A teacher decides that students need a break from the challenging economics curriculum and decides to engage the class in a game of Jeopardy. Immediately, the students are excited as they divide themselves into teams and begin responding to the various items across the different answer categories unrelated to economics. Although the students enjoy playing the game, the students do not deepen their understanding of the economics vocabulary.

⊘ What It Is

Checking in an ongoing manner to ensure that connections are effective

Example: A teacher decides to make reading class more interesting by engaging students in comparing/contrasting the story they are reading to a popular television show. Before the teacher gives the assignment, she asks students questions about the television show and learns that few students have seen it. She then modifies her plan by asking students to discuss television shows that have similar story lines to the story they are reading. As almost all students relate story lines from one particular television show, the teacher gives an assignment asking students to compare and contrast a story line from that particular show with the story they are reading.

(X) What It Isn't

Assuming that lessons intended to create a connection with students will succeed in doing so

Example: A teacher decides to make reading class more interesting by engaging students in comparing/contrasting the story they are reading to a popular television show. Students begin work on the assignment; however, only a few of the students have ever seen the new television show. The teacher assumes that the lack of quality responses is due to students' difficulties understanding the concepts *compare* and *contrast*.

Practice Guide Related to Culturally, Socially, and Personally Responsive Teaching

For information on possible uses of this practice guide, please see page xiii in the Preface.

Table 4.1

1.	Was the lesson designed to include elements that students in the class were likely to perceive as related to their cultural backgrounds?	Y	N
2.	Was the lesson designed to include elements that the students in the class were likely to perceive as related to their social or personal backgrounds?	Y	N
3.	Did the teacher explain concepts in ways that helped students relate?	Y	N
4.	Did the teacher include content that broadened what students were learning so students were more likely to find the lesson relevant to their lives?		
5.	Did the teacher use instructional strategies that built upon the cultural, social, and personal strengths of the students served?		
6.	Were lesson activities designed in ways that engaged all students actively?	Y	N
7.	Did the teacher differentiate aspects of the lesson to increase the likelihood that all students would engage and be more likely to understand?	Y	N
8.	If students did not understand, did the teacher modify examples?	Y	N
9.	If students mastered concepts early, did the teacher offer a higher level of challenge?	Y	N

In a strong lesson, a "yes" answer is recorded for at least five of these items.
In an outstanding lesson, a "yes" answer is recorded for at least seven of these items.

Practical Next Steps ☼

1. In collaboration with teacher colleagues, engage in a book study of *Culturally Responsive Teaching and the Brain: Promoting Authentic Engagement and Rigor Among Culturally and Linguistically Diverse Students* (Hammond, 2015; in particular, read Chapters 1–4).

2. In collaboration with teacher colleagues, identify the racial, ethnic, or linguistic groups of students who traditionally have not succeeded in your classes. Determine what strategies you can employ to get to know those students better. In particular, determine how you will go about learning what interests, motivates, and excites those students. Schedule a date to report back to your colleagues and discuss what you have learned.

3. With the colleagues in your grade-level team or subject-area team, select a learning objective that students did not master well. Together, design a set of lessons that have a higher likelihood of helping the diverse groups of students you teach develop a deep understanding of the learning objective. In particular, consider how you can build lessons that take advantage of what you know about the students' cultures and their social and personal backgrounds, experiences, and interests in ways that will help students better understand what you want them to learn. After implementing the lessons, examine student work together using success criteria you developed. Determine what practices might have been useful in advancing understanding. Determine what practices might be improved to generate higher levels of understanding.

References

Chiles, N. (2018, October 4). *How "The Walking Dead" helps Revere High School make the grade*. New York, NY: Hechinger Report.

Delpit, L. (2005). *Other people's children: Cultural conflict in the classroom* (2nd ed.). New York: The New Press.

Gay, G. (2010). *Culturally responsive teaching: Theory, research, and practice* (2nd ed.). New York: Teachers College Press.

Germain-McCarthy, Y., & Owens, K. (2005). *Mathematics and multi-ethnic students: Exemplary practices*. Larchmont, NY: Eye On Education.

Ginsberg, M. B., & Wlodkowski, R. J. (2000). *Creating highly motivating classrooms for all students: A schoolwide approach to powerful teaching with diverse learners*. San Francisco, CA: Jossey-Bass.

Hammond, Z. L. (2015). *Culturally responsive teaching and the brain: Promoting authentic engagement and rigor among culturally and linguistically diverse students*. Thousand Oaks, CA: Sage.

Howard, T. (2001). Powerful pedagogy for African American students: A case study of four teachers. *Urban Education, 36*(2), 179–202.

Ladson-Billings, G. (2009). *The dreamkeepers: Successful teachers for African American children* (2nd ed.). San Francisco, CA: Jossey-Bass.

Reyes, P., Scribner, J. D., & Scribner, A. P. (1999). *Lessons from high-performing Hispanic schools*. New York: Teachers College Press.

Tomlinson, C. A. (1999). *The differentiated classroom: Responding to the needs of all learners*. Alexandria, VA: Association for Supervision and Curriculum Development.

Wiggins, G. P., & McTighe, J. (2005). *Understanding by design* (Expanded 2nd ed.). Upper Saddle River, NJ: Pearson Education, Inc.

Checking Understanding, Providing Feedback, and Adapting

5

In a fourth-grade classroom at Branch Brook School in Newark, New Jersey, students worked busily in small groups pursuing their reading assignment. Each group had the task of reading a novel and creating a book review. Every student had a specific role that was essential to the group's success, so everyone had to be involved. The teacher floated from group to group, listening to student conversations about the important items for inclusion in the review. One student had the important job of asking questions that the book review should address. As the student asked questions, the other students attempted to answer. Students did not always agree, but they had learned to support their answers through the text, providing evidence for their answers from the novel.

When the teacher saw that one student was responding less often than others, the teacher asked the student, "What do you think? Do you agree or disagree? Why?" or some similar question, both to make the student think and to place the student back in the thick of the conversation. If a student had difficulty answering, the teacher probed in a manner that helped the student use prior knowledge, relate, consider alternatives, or otherwise move closer to understanding the important aspects of the novel.

In this case, the teacher was listening to hear what students understood and what they did not understand. He interacted with students in ways that helped to bring the novel to life in each child's mind. His questions led each student to identify and understand various story elements and perceive how the author had pursued and accomplished his purpose. The depth and quality of the conversation made it clear that some students had achieved this level of understanding. The teacher, however, wanted every student to demonstrate this level of understanding, either through the conversation among his or her peers or through the teacher's careful probing.

Branch Brook School is in the Newark Public Schools in Newark, New Jersey. The school serves approximately 170 students in grades pre-kindergarten through four. The school won the America's Best Urban Schools Award in 2010.

A Perpetual Question

On the Minds of Educators Striving to Produce Equity and Excellence

How can I get each and every one of my students to believe, "My teacher knows how I am understanding this concept right now and is continuously giving me feedback to guide me toward mastery"?

In high-performing urban schools, teachers seek abundant evidence that students understand the concepts and skills being taught. To promote mastery of a specific concept, teachers frequently check to determine if their students have acquired meaning from the information shared in the prior few minutes. Teachers rarely assume that students understand. Instead, they look for evidence of understanding in oral responses, written responses, or other performances or demonstrations. This checking for understanding occurs with much greater frequency than it does in more typical schools. In typical schools, teachers might ask a few questions at the end of the chapter or lesson. In contrast, teachers in high-performing urban schools ask questions continuously. Also, in typical schools, checking for understanding is often limited to a few students (the ones who raise their hands to respond), whereas in high-performing urban schools, teachers check all or almost all students to ensure that everyone makes progress in mastering the lesson content. Furthermore, in high-performing urban schools, checking for understanding is purposeful and strategic. Teachers do not ask questions simply because the teacher's guide makes the suggestion or because the principal is watching. Instead, teachers check because they want accurate information about students' levels of understanding so they can respond by adjusting instruction accordingly.

In high-performing urban schools, when students respond, teachers provide feedback that acknowledges students' engagement, reinforces their understanding, guides their thinking toward better and deeper understandings, and communicates that they are both valued and capable. As illustrated in Figure 5.1, the practice of checking understanding and providing feedback contributes both to a focus on understanding and mastery and to a focus on ensuring that every student feels valued and capable.

Checking understanding and providing feedback is high-quality formative assessment. It is not an event (such as giving a semester test) as much as it is a way of teaching. Effective teaching practices help teachers continuously know how their students are making sense of what they are teaching. Fisher and Frey (2007) explained that teachers can use a wide array of questioning techniques, writing tasks, projects, performances, and tests to acquire high-quality information about what students understand, misunderstand, or have yet to understand. In the high-performing urban schools we studied, teachers checked students' understandings frequently, they examined what each student understood, and they checked to ensure that students were developing deep understandings of concepts. As well, based on student responses, teachers provided high-quality feedback, and they adapted their teaching, modified their examples, reframed their questions, highlighted different connections, and guided students closer to mastery of the content they needed to learn.

Frequency of Checking for Understanding

In most classrooms in high-performing urban schools, student voices are heard more frequently than teacher voices. Teachers spend less time presenting. They spend more time trying to determine what students understand. Teachers present new information but then check almost immediately to determine if students heard, processed, and internalized the information accurately. Continually and persistently, teachers in high-performing schools check: Does this student understand? Does this make sense to her? Can he relate to this? Can she explain this in her own words?

In typical classrooms, teachers might lecture for ten, twenty, thirty minutes or longer before asking students questions. In contrast, in high-performing urban schools, teachers are asking questions every few minutes and in some cases, every few seconds. A teacher at William Dandy Middle School in Fort Lauderdale, Florida, offered her rationale for her frequent questioning by explaining, "I am assessing all the time. I need to know if my students are with me or not. I don't let them fall behind, not even for a minute."

Often teachers in high-performing urban schools develop systems that allow them to check every student's level of understanding efficiently. For example, some teachers give students individual white boards and markers and expect them to write responses to a question. A teacher might say, "Write on your white board a mathematical sentence that illustrates this story. Don't show your answer until I ask you to do so." Then, at the teacher's signal, everyone raises their white board and shows their work. The teacher can quickly look at every response and determine if all, most, a few, or no students answered correctly. This type of approach challenges all students to respond and allows the teacher to gauge the progress of students who have varying academic strengths and needs.

In some classrooms, teachers acquire evidence of understanding by asking students to respond in unison. In these situations, teachers ask a question and then listen closely for variations in answers. We have also observed teachers listening carefully and noticing which student or students did not respond simultaneously with the group. For example, when the kindergarten teacher at C.E. Rose Elementary in Tucson, Arizona, did not hear every student answer her call for a group response, she said, "I didn't hear Alejandro's row," in a manner that prompted every student to participate fully.

Frequently, teachers will follow up by calling upon students who were slow to answer and asking them to respond individually. Thus, the unison response should be more than a rote drill or a routine script. In high-performing urban schools, teachers use unison responses efficiently and effectively to determine that all students understand the information presented.

At Ira Harbison Elementary in San Diego, California (National School District), teachers used electronic clickers as a way of eliciting quick feedback about students' levels of understanding. Students frequently used their clickers to "vote" for answers that appeared on the electronic Smart Board. The technology allowed

Figure 5.1

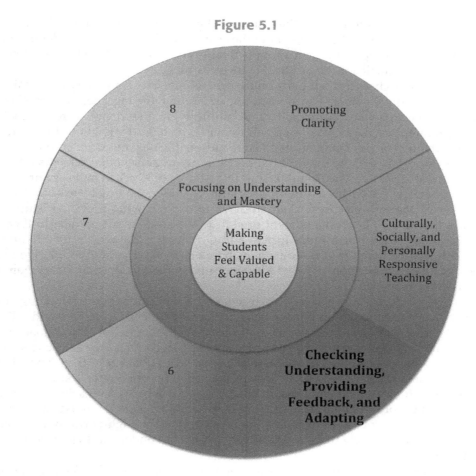

teachers to determine which students answered correctly or incorrectly and adapt their instruction accordingly.

In many classrooms, teachers check for understanding by asking students to write short responses. As students write sentences or paragraphs, teachers rapidly circulate throughout the classroom observing what students are writing. Teachers watch students as they perform, allowing teachers to immediately see errors in student thinking. Often, teachers quickly determine which students understand and which students need additional support.

In high-performing elementary, middle, and high schools, we observed teachers checking for understanding by engaging students in group discussions focused upon the lesson objective. Teachers stimulated discussion with thought-provoking, sometimes controversial questions and then carefully monitored the discussion that followed. If discussion occurred in small groups, teachers rotated from group to group and listened to determine if students understood the key concepts associated with the lesson objective.

At R. N. Harris Integrated Arts/Core Knowledge School in Durham, North Carolina, a second-grade teacher used games that required students to work in teams in order to answer questions about the history and geography of China. While all students participated in deliberations about the answers to the questions, students took turns writing and reporting their group's final responses. As a result, all students were held accountable for demonstrating their learning.

Although teachers in high-performing urban schools use a variety of teaching strategies to acquire evidence of student understanding, the most common method appears to be frequent questions, targeted to individual students. Through their active probing, teachers create a climate within which students know they must remain attentive or risk being unprepared to answer the next question posed.

It is important to note that in high-performing urban schools, teachers refuse to accept silence as evidence of understanding. Rarely (if ever), in high-performing urban schools, did we hear teachers check student understanding by asking, "Any questions?" Instead, teachers asked students to explain what they had learned, discuss the details, teach the content or skill to the student sitting next to them, write a letter to describe a procedure to a friend, draw a diagram of the relationship between two concepts, or engage in some other activity that would give the teacher a clear indication of what students understood and what unanswered questions remained.

In high-performing urban schools, teachers checked student understanding not simply as a routine or a compliance behavior but as a means to understand what students were thinking. Thus, we observed teachers asking frequent questions and taking time to listen carefully to student responses. In contrast, some teachers ask questions without listening intently to student responses (Black & Wiliam, 1998). For example, some teachers proceed to answer their own question after waiting only a few seconds for a student response. In other cases, a teacher fails to acknowledge a student's appropriate response, because the teacher had a predetermined, more limited notion of the correct answer. Teachers we observed in high-performing urban schools were more likely to listen attentively in order to understand what their students were thinking.

Many teachers think of formative assessment as pen or pencil tasks, completed at the end of the week or at end of a unit of instruction, for the purpose of generating a grade. In contrast, in high-performing urban schools, formative assessments happen continuously for the primary purpose of improving learning. Teachers are always seeking to know specifically what students understand and are yet to understand so that they can shape their instruction in ways that generate greater learning. In discussing formative assessment, Stiggins (2005) explained that teachers should use assessment not simply as a means to report learning results but as a tool to improve teaching in ways that will generate better learning results. In the schools we studied, we found teachers modeling this type of formative assessment, consistently and continuously, in ways that promoted student mastery.

Well-Distributed Checking for Understanding

Nuthall (2005) discussed how some educators tend to cling to the belief that telling and teaching are the same thing; that what works in face-to-face conversation will work with a class of twenty to thirty students; and that attending only to head nodding, eye contact, and facial expressions will provide sufficient evidence of understanding. Consequently, as Nuthall explained, "Teachers depend on the responses of a small number of key students as indicators and remain ignorant of what most of the class knows and understands" (p. 920).

By checking the understanding of all their students, teachers in high-performing urban schools help ensure equitable and excellent learning outcomes. Black, Latino, Native American, and Southeast Asian students, students with emerging bilingualism, students with disabilities, and students from other groups that traditionally are not served well achieve deeper levels of understanding and mastery, in part because teachers purposefully check their understanding.

Almost fifty years ago, Good and Brophy (1971) found that teachers were less likely to call upon and check the understanding of students they perceived as low achievers. Similarly, Good and Brophy (1972) found that teachers were more likely to call upon and check the understanding of students with whom they felt attachment. To achieve equitable learning outcomes, "Teachers need to know which students are and are not engaged in thinking about the instructional objective being taught" (McKenzie & Skrla, 2011, p. 43). McKenzie and Skrla (2011) maintained that teachers do this by assessing the active cognitive engagement of all their students.

In high-performing urban schools, teachers try to ensure that all students have abundant opportunities to respond to questions. They want evidence that each and every student is making progress toward developing deeper levels of understanding. Teachers acquire such evidence through both their question-posing strategies and their careful attention to the responses of each student.

Of course, when teachers use any of the group response strategies described previously, they give all students opportunities to respond. For example, when teachers ask students to solve a problem on their individual white boards, they give every student an opportunity to complete the problem and then quickly check each student's response. In a more typical class, a teacher might ask one student at a time to come to the classroom board and solve a problem. While one student responds, other students may disengage. Furthermore, when teachers use such one-student-at-a-time strategies, only a few students might have an opportunity to share. Consequently, the teacher has little or no information to determine if the other students understand the concept or skill.

In high-performing urban schools, teachers distribute opportunities to respond even when they do not use group response strategies. Commonly, these teachers call upon students before they raise their hands. In some cases, teachers draw student names randomly to ensure evenly distributed response opportunities. In other classrooms, teachers use a class roster or grade book to record student responses as students answer questions. Generally speaking, however, teachers in high-performing urban schools do not restrict their questioning to a strategy whereby students raise their hands to be called upon. Randomly, sequentially, or strategically, they acknowledge students in a manner that offers all students opportunities to respond. Likewise, in some classrooms, teachers achieve the same even distribution of response opportunities by allowing students to call upon each other. For example, in an English class at Kearny School of International Business in San Diego, California, a student answered the teacher's question about the memoir the class was reading, *The Glass Castle*, and then asked another student to offer additional or contradictory evidence from the memoir. Sometimes the teacher called upon students, and at other times, the teacher allowed students to call upon each other, intending to ensure that every student contributed to the conversation.

At Kearny School of International Business, as in other high-performing urban schools, students were not ignored when they sat quietly and passively. The school's principal explained, "Students here are not allowed to sit quietly and fail. That's unacceptable." Instead, all students were expected to participate actively in class discussions. They were challenged to respond to questions in ways that demonstrated their level of understanding.

The thorough distribution of response opportunities in high-performing urban school classrooms may help explain why certain student populations achieve much better results than are typical. For example, students with emerging bilingualism, students of color, students with disabilities, or students with behavior challenges are not allowed to sit quietly and wait for the class period to end. Teachers engage these students in answering questions at least as much as they engage other students. Students learn that they are expected to learn. Students know that each day, in each class, they will be called upon to participate, engage, and demonstrate their understanding.

Checking for Higher Levels of Understanding

In high-performing urban schools, teachers strive to ensure all students are able to answer questions that require high levels of cognitive ability. All students are expected to learn the lesson objective and demonstrate a depth of knowledge that extends beyond surface-level recall. Thus, teachers will ask many questions that require students to compare, contrast, explain, describe, infer, analyze, and evaluate. And yet pushing for higher levels of understanding is not the same as asking questions students find impossible to answer. In high-performing urban schools, teachers work to build students' capacity to respond to challenging questions. For example, teachers may ensure that students first master more basic concepts before they pursue more complex ones. Teachers may pursue lower levels of understanding before asking questions that require deeper levels of cognitive demand.

Good and Brophy (1973) reported that teachers may not distribute opportunities to answer higher-order thinking questions equitably. Teachers may intentionally or unintentionally ask more complex questions to students perceived as more capable. As well, students perceived as less capable may receive more questions that only require the recall of simple facts. The authors explained that denying students opportunities to respond to challenging questions limited students' opportunities to learn and grow.

In high-performing urban schools, we observed teachers utilizing a variety of strategies to check the depth of their students' understanding. Through one commonly used strategy, teachers engaged students in rich discussions about the concepts being taught. At schools like Finney Elementary in Chula Vista, California; McLean Middle School in Fort Worth, Texas; and the Middle College at UNCG in Greensboro, North Carolina, we observed teachers engaging all of their students in discussions that required the students to think deeply about what they had learned. Black and Wiliam (1998) emphasized how strategically structured discussions can increase students' understanding of their own thinking as well as help teachers understand the depth of students' understanding.

In schools such as Maplewood Richmond Heights High School in St. Louis, Missouri; Eastwood Middle School in El Paso, Texas; and Highland Elementary in Silver

Springs, Maryland, we saw teachers provoke student engagement in discussions by asking questions with an element of controversy. Teachers required students to utilize what they had read to support their arguments.

In many elementary schools such as Fay Herron Elementary in Las Vegas, Spring Creek Elementary in Garland, Texas, and Lauderbach Elementary in Chula Vista, California, we observed teachers using guided reading groups as opportunities to engage students in deep conversations. Teachers utilized these small-group settings to probe students' thinking and encourage students to discuss how they understood important issues and concepts related to their reading.

In high-performing urban schools, teachers differentiated the questions they posed to students as another important strategy for maximizing student engagement with challenging academic content. Students were more likely to invest effort in listening and participating when they knew they would be called upon to answer a question that was challenging yet targeted to their current level of skill or need. For example, in a kindergarten class at Golden Empire Elementary in Sacramento, California, the teacher gave students turns blending together three or four letter sounds and then reading the one-syllable word. The teacher prompted each child to say the sounds in the word, blend the sounds together, and then read the word quickly. The students found the task challenging; however, most succeeded on the first try. When the teacher gave Maria a turn, the teacher picked a more difficult one-syllable word and did not prompt Maria to say the sounds first. Maria immediately read the word correctly. Through this small, subtle adaptation of content and process, the teacher acknowledged Maria's ability, gave her an opportunity to practice at a level that was appropriately challenging, and kept Maria highly engaged throughout the lesson.

At Wynnebrook Elementary in West Palm Beach, Florida, teachers credited a large part of the school's success to the use of differentiated instruction in all subject areas. For example, during literacy instruction, additional teachers are in classrooms to help ensure that all students are being challenged appropriately as they work toward higher levels of understanding. In many high-performing urban schools, teachers differentiate tasks by adjusting the cognitive complexity of the questions they ask. Other teachers differentiate by asking a student to answer a question that was answered correctly by another student a few minutes prior. Teachers might also differentiate by varying the details of the prompts provided. For example, a teacher might ask one student to describe a procedure, another student to explain an application of the procedure to a real-life situation, and yet another student to discern if there might be another way to approach the problem. In another classroom, a teacher might call upon one student to answer a challenging question and then call upon a struggling student to answer a very similar question, slightly restated. All of these approaches might address the same learning objective while providing all students opportunities to advance toward higher levels of understanding.

Providing Feedback

Teachers in high-performing urban schools are eager to learn what their students understand as well as what they may not yet understand. Teachers often probe to validate their assumptions about what students know and do not know. Importantly, teachers keep their specific learning objective in mind, because they want to know how each student is progressing toward understanding the specific concept or skill. For example, if the objective requires students to analyze the findings from an experiment, the teacher may ultimately ask questions that demand analysis of complex information; however, en route to such an objective, the teacher may seek to ensure that students are mastering the details and concepts they will need to perform complex analyses later.

As teachers listen and watch, they respond to students in ways that help students move closer to mastery of the objective. In particular, in high-performing urban schools, teachers frequently provided feedback in ways that respectfully corrected misconceptions and affirmed accurate responses. Teachers provided feedback in ways that helped students know their teachers valued them and wanted them to master the learning objective.

Hattie (2009) reported that the provision of feedback can be one of the most powerful influences on student learning. However, not just any feedback will do. High-quality feedback addresses both cognitive factors (information students need to understand where they are en route to mastering a concept) and motivational factors (information that helps students feel they are capable of mastering the concept; Brookhart, 2008). Stiggins (2005) explained that when students have continual access to substantive feedback about their learning, they can set goals, watch their progress, and develop confidence that their continued success is possible. With abundant, high-quality feedback, students are able to make meaning by using and controlling their own thought processes (Brookhart, 2008).

In our visits to high-performing urban schools, we saw teachers providing abundant, high-quality feedback that helped students gauge their progress toward understanding and mastery, simultaneously helping students know that they were both valued and capable of achieving mastery. Typically, we observed teachers reinforcing correct answers, acknowledging students for their attention, thinking, creativity, and effort. We observed teachers providing high-quality feedback that helped students realize and appreciate what they did correctly. As well, when students answered incorrectly, teachers helped unpack students' thinking so students might understand where or how they erred.

The teachers we observed in high-performing schools were never punitive in their responses. Teacher feedback was prompt, clear, and respectful. Teachers corrected misconceptions in ways that helped students better understand challenging concepts. Students knew they could take risks and try to answer difficult questions, because their teachers would not embarrass or humiliate them. They trusted that their teacher was committed to helping them learn, understand, and master the lesson's objective.

For example, in one school, we saw a teacher challenge a student's incorrect answer with a question designed to prompt the student to rethink a misconception. When a student explained that the reason temperatures were hotter in summer and colder in winter was the earth's greater proximity to the sun during summer, the teacher asked, "But, if that's true, how it could it be hotter in one hemisphere (summer) and colder in the other (winter) at the same time?" The student recognized that something was wrong with his answer and listened more attentively as the teacher continued to probe and guide students to understand that the tilt of the earth's axis had a major influence on seasonal temperatures.

Importantly, teachers in high-performing schools created positive classroom cultures in which students supported and encouraged each other to engage and respond. Teachers modeled appreciation of students' desire to learn, their courage to respond to difficult questions, and their efforts to deepen their understandings. In elementary, middle, and high schools, teachers created safe places where students felt comfortable sharing their own ideas as well as asking their own questions about skills and concepts they had not yet mastered.

Adapting Instruction

Throughout lessons, teachers continually made decisions about instruction based upon their perceptions of student understanding. In other words, while the teacher's feedback influenced students' thinking, the answers provided by students and the questions students asked influenced the teacher's decisions about how the lesson should proceed. As a result of their efforts to check student understanding, teachers decided what students might need to see, hear, touch, or experience next to advance closer to mastering the lesson objective. As described in the previous chapter, often, teachers tried to adapt their presentation of a concept in a manner that better connected to the interests, backgrounds, learning styles, prior experiences, or culture of the students they serve.

In addition to adapting lesson content, teachers sometimes altered the pace of instruction based upon the feedback they garner from students. If student responses indicated high levels of mastery, teachers might accelerate their pace. Conversely, if students seemed confused, teachers might adapt by slowing their progression from one concept to the next.

In addition to making adaptations within lessons, teachers also adapted subsequent lessons based upon student responses. In many high-performing urban schools, we observed teachers using end-of-lesson checks or exit tickets to gauge the extent of student understanding. In some cases, the exit ticket was a set of oral responses to teacher questions. In some cases, the exit ticket required students to demonstrate or model a response. In others, the exit ticket required a short written response. The exit ticket helped the teacher know how to adapt the plan for the next day's instruction in order to build upon student levels of understanding. If student responses indicated high levels of mastery of the day's specific objective, the teacher might plan the following lesson to address the next more challenging objective. If exit-ticket responses indicated a lack of understanding, teachers might use the information to help define specifically what students understood and what they did not understand. In accordance with this information, the next lesson and/or subsequent individual student interventions might be focused in a manner that built upon existing understandings while addressing the very specific content students still needed to learn.

For example, a teacher might use four word problems requiring subtraction as an exit ticket for her math lesson. Students might respond to each question by writing the number sentence associated with each word problem, calculating an answer, and then writing an explanation of each answer. By watching and noting student responses, the teacher might determine that all but three students answered all aspects of three of the four questions correctly. Also, the teacher might notice that half of the students answered the problem that required regrouping across zeros incorrectly. In response, the teacher might plan to devote the next lesson to word problems that require regrouping across zeros. Additionally, the teacher might plan a focused intervention session with the three students who needed additional assistance.

Summary

One might easily be impressed with the high-performing urban schools we studied simply by looking at end-of-year assessment results that reveal remarkable learning results for almost every student. On the other hand, when visiting classrooms in high-performing urban schools, an up-close examination reveals remarkable daily learning results for almost every student. In high-performing urban schools, learning is not an annual phenomenon. It is a daily, hourly, or even minute-to-minute phenomenon. One reason for the remarkable daily learning results observed is the frequent, well-distributed checking for understanding that occurs in classrooms throughout each high-performing urban school. Much of teachers' checking for understanding focuses upon challenging concepts and higher-order thinking skills. Another reason for strong daily learning results is the frequent, high-quality feedback teachers provide to all of their students. Teachers provide feedback in a manner that both motivates students and helps students understand where they are en route to mastering the learning objective. Finally, teachers promote strong daily learning results by adapting their teaching in response to the answers provided by students. Constantly, teachers decide what they will do next based on the information students provide about what they understand and what they are yet to understand.

In other words, by checking understanding, providing feedback continuously, and adapting instruction accordingly, teachers in high-performing urban schools make sure that every student makes learning progress each day. Furthermore, teachers in these schools check understanding, provide feedback, and adapt instruction for all of their students, without regard to prior knowledge, race, ethnicity, language background, or any other factor. Teachers make sure all students engage, learn, benefit from feedback, and advance toward mastering the content being taught that day. In high-performing urban schools, minute-to-minute learning added up to daily learning, which added up to impressive annual learning gains for all students.

What It Is & What It Isn't

Checking Understanding, Providing Feedback, and Adapting

✓ What It Is

Checking to determine students' level of understanding frequently

> Example: As the teacher tries to help students understand the relationship between the earth's revolution around the sun and the four seasons, the teacher presents one PowerPoint slide that illustrates the tilt of the earth's axis toward the sun during summer and then asks students a series of questions: Where is it going to be summer in this picture? Why? Where is it going to be winter in this picture? Why? Will the days be longer or shorter in the Northern Hemisphere? Why? Then the teacher asks one student to stand and act out the role of the sun and asks another to hold a Styrofoam model of the earth with a pencil axis. The teacher asks the students to model summer. Next, the teacher asks other students the same series of questions. After asking at least a dozen questions, the teacher progresses to the next PowerPoint slide, illustrating the tilt of the earth's axis away from the sun during winter. Again, the teacher poses a similar set of questions.

✗ What It Isn't

Infrequently checking to gauge students' understanding

> Example: The teacher shows a PowerPoint presentation intended to explain the relationship between the earth's revolution around the sun and the four seasons. With each PowerPoint slide, the teacher offers a three-minute lecture that discusses issues related to the tilt of the earth's axis, the earth's distance from the sun, and the differential impact on the hemispheres, the equator, and the poles. At the conclusion of the lecture, the teacher asks students to answer questions about the seasons.

✓ What It Is

Checking each and every student's level of understanding

> Example: In a middle school math class, a teacher presents x-y graphs that illustrate hourly wages, hours worked, and bonuses earned. The teacher organizes students into small teams of three and designates each student as Student A, B, or C. The teacher asks the students to work with their teammates to explain what the graph implies about salaries. Then the teacher asks Student B in each group to stand and explain the graph to their team. Next, the teacher asks each Student A to answer specific questions about data points on the graph (e.g., How much did this person earn

and why?). Finally, the teacher asks each Student C to explain how the graph would change if either the hourly rate changed or the bonus changed.

⊗ What It Isn't

Checking only a few students' understanding

> Example: In a middle school math class, a teacher presents x-y graphs that illustrate hourly wages, hours worked, and bonuses earned. The teacher presents each graph and asks questions about specific data points, trend lines, and so on. A few students raise their hands or blurt out answers. The teacher calls upon the students who want to participate in the conversation. Other students sit quietly and wait for the period to end.

⊘ What It Is

Checking for higher levels of understanding

> Example: As students sit in a circle and read *Charlotte's Web*, the teacher asks a variety of questions intended to promote thinking about cause-and-effect relationships. For example, the teacher asks, "Why were the animals worried about Wilbur? What did the animals think would happen if Charlotte wrote words over Wilbur's head?" Then the teacher asks students to share the cause-and-effect questions they wrote on sticky notes as they read the chapter. As students read their questions, the teacher guides students in considering if the question examines cause–effect relationships. Then the teacher invites students to answer the question using specific evidence from the text.

⊗ What It Isn't

Asking questions that require only the recall of facts

> Example: As students read *Charlotte's Web*, the teacher asks students multiple questions about details in the story (e.g., Who was Charlotte? Where did Fern live? What was the first word Charlotte wrote in her web?).

⊘ What It Is

Providing feedback that advances student understanding

> Example: When a student answers that condensation occurs when water falls from the sky, the teacher probes by asking the student to describe the other two parts of the water cycle. The student accurately specifies and explains both evaporation and precipitation. While explaining precipitation, the student realizes that her explanation of condensation was identical to her explanation of precipitation.

"Oops. So, I guess condensation must be something else." The teacher affirms the student's conclusion and says, "I'm going to ask Javier what he thinks condensation is, but then I'm going to come back to you with another question about condensation."

(X) What It Isn't

Providing feedback that does not help students know what they understand correctly and what they are yet to understand

> Example: When a student answers that condensation occurs when water falls from the sky, the teacher turns to another student and asks, "What is condensation?"

(✓) What It Is

Providing feedback that motivates students to stay engaged and maximize their effort

> Example: When a student cites language from the history textbook to answer a question about the solutions political parties posed to address the Great Depression, the teacher acknowledges that the student did an excellent job finding a passage that describes how political parties assigned blame for the Great Depression. The teacher encourages the student to look for a passage that describes the solutions political parties were suggesting.

(X) What It Isn't

Providing feedback in ways that cause students to stop trying

> Example: When a student cites language from the history textbook to answer a question about the solutions political parties posed to address the Great Depression, the teacher responds, "That isn't even close to what I was asking. You obviously aren't paying attention!"

(✓) What It Is

Observing students' levels of understanding and adapting instruction accordingly

> Example: In Spanish class, the teacher engages students in conjugating the present tense of the verb *hablar* (to speak). While students successfully repeat the conjugation, several students respond incorrectly when the teacher asks them to explain why they need to know how to conjugate the verb. Then the teacher strays from her planned activity and writes the word *speaks* on the board. She asks the students to generate different sentences that correctly employ the verb. Next, she asks students why none of them offered sentences that started with *I speaks* or *We speaks*. Students laugh

and explain that it would not have been proper English. The teacher then explains how verb conjugations in English follow general rules, just as verb conjugations in Spanish follow general rules.

Ⓧ What It Isn't

Ignoring information about student misconceptions

Example: In Spanish class, the teacher engages students in conjugating the present tense of the verb *hablar* (to speak). While students successfully repeat the conjugation, several students respond incorrectly when the teacher asks them to explain why they need to know how to conjugate the verb. The teacher hears the incorrect answers but does not want to take the time to explain. She continues with the conjugation of the next Spanish verb.

Practice Guide Related to Checking Understanding, Providing Feedback, and Adapting

For information on possible uses of this practice guide, please see page xiii in the Preface.

Which strategies did the teacher use to check student understanding?

- Posing questions for individual student oral responses
- Posing questions for group oral responses
- Inviting students to answer questions with hand signals
- Using electronic clickers to collect and analyze student responses
- Leading and observing students in Socratic seminars
- Observing dialogue among pairs or small groups of students
- Using individual student white boards
- Using writing to check for understanding
- Observing students engaging in projects
- Observing students perform
- Observing student presentations
- Using common formative assessments
- Using exit tickets
- Other: _____

Did the strategies utilized provide the teacher with perspective about the understanding of all students? Most students? Few students? Which strategies most effectively engaged which students? _____

_____

What strategies might the teacher employ to maximize information about each and every student's understanding? _____

_____

What evidence suggests that the strategies employed helped the teacher understand the extent to which students were developing deep understandings of the learning objective? _____

_____

How might strategies be modified to increase the teacher's acquisition of information about each student's depth of understanding?

_____

_____

How did the teacher provide students feedback? Which students received high-quality feedback that was both motivational and informative?

_____

_____

What might the teacher do to provide more students high-quality feedback? _____

_____

How did the teacher adapt instruction in response to evidence of student understanding? _____

_____

Practical Next Steps

1. In collaboration with teacher colleagues, engage in a book study of *Checking for Understanding* (Fisher & Frey, 2007). Each chapter provides useful examples of opportunities to strengthen checking for understanding. Determine which strategies could be utilized to increase (1) the frequency of checking for understanding, (2) the distribution of checking for understanding among all students, and (3) the depth of student understanding examined.

2. At the end of a lesson, review your class roster and make notes about which students you believe developed a strong understanding of the

concept you were teaching. Ask yourself what evidence supports your beliefs about each student's level of understanding. Plan how you will check your assumptions during the next lesson.

3. Ask a colleague to observe the feedback you provide to students during a lesson. Ask the colleague to write down your responses as precisely as possible. In debriefing with the colleague, first note the quantity of feedback. Was the amount of feedback sufficient to help students understand how their learning was progressing toward the lesson objective? Next, note the distribution of the feedback. Was the feedback distributed evenly to all students in the class? Next, look at the motivational aspect of the feedback you provided. Was your feedback likely to encourage students to remain engaged and think hard? Or might your feedback have negatively influenced the engagement of some students? Finally, look at the informational aspect of your feedback. Did your feedback give students information that helped them know what they were understanding, what they were not yet understanding, or where they were en route to understanding? Offer to conduct the same type of observation for your colleague.

References

Black, P., & Wiliam, D. (1998). Inside the black box: Raising standards through classroom assessment. *Phi Delta Kappan, 80*(2), 139–149.

Brookhart, S. M. (2008). *How to give effective feedback to your students.* Alexandria, VA: Association for Supervision and Curriculum Development.

Fisher, D., & Frey, N. (2007). *Checking for understanding: Formative assessment techniques for your classroom.* Alexandria, VA: Association for Supervision and Curriculum Development.

Good, T. L., & Brophy, J. E. (1971). Analyzing classroom interaction: A more powerful alternative. *Educational Technology, 11,* 36–41.

Good, T. L., & Brophy, J. E. (1972). Behavioral expression of teacher attitudes. *Journal of Educational Psychology, 63,* 617–624.

Good, T. L., & Brophy, J. E. (1973). *Looking into classrooms.* New York: Harper & Row.

Hattie, J. (2009). *Visible learning: A synthesis of over 800 meta-analyses relating to achievement.* New York, NY: Routledge.

McKenzie, K. B., & Skrla, L. (2011). *Using equity audits in the classroom to reach and teach all students.* Thousand Oaks, CA: Corwin.

Nuthall, G. (2005). The cultural myths and realities of classroom teaching and learning: A personal journey. *Teachers College Record, 107*(5), 895–934.

Stiggins, R. (2005). From formative assessment to assessment for learning: A path to success in standards-based schools. *Phi Delta Kappan, 87*(4), 324–328.

6 Building Fluency With Gatekeeper Vocabulary

At Rose Park Math and Science Magnet School in Nashville, Tennessee, a science teacher led a lab in which the middle school's students were learning a strategy for extracting DNA. The teacher explained the process for extracting DNA from fruit and the reasons for doing so. He engaged the students in the lab process and began circulating among the students. "So, what are you doing?" the teacher asked one of the students.

"We're extracting the DNA from these strawberries," the student explained.

"What does 'extracting' mean?" the teacher asked, as if he had never heard the term.

"Well, extracting means getting something out or separating it," the student responded.

"Good," the teacher commented as he approached the next student and asked, "Why would anyone want to extract DNA?"

The teacher was checking to ensure that students accurately performed the procedure; however, the teacher was equally interested in ensuring that students could discuss and explain the procedure.

> Rose Park Math and Science Magnet Middle School is in the Metropolitan Nashville Public Schools in Nashville, Tennessee. The school serves 440 students in grades five through eight. Rose Park won the America's Best Urban School Award in 2013 and again in 2017.

In a third-grade class at E.A. "Squatty" Lyons Elementary School in Houston, Texas, the teacher explained to her class that they would learn a new strategy for multiplying called "partial products." She explained the process, one step at a time. With each step, the teacher engaged students in discussing the step with the child sitting next to them. Once students had experienced the entire strategy, the teacher asked students to work in pairs to solve 54 times 3. After providing a couple of minutes for the students to solve the problem, the teacher asked the students in each pair to take turns explaining the entire process to their partner. The teacher circulated throughout the classroom and listened to the students. Every student was able to explain how to use the partial products strategy correctly.

> E.A. "Squatty" Lyons Elementary is in the Houston Independent School District in Houston, Texas. The school serves 1,000 students in preschool through fifth grade. The school won the America's Best Urban School Award in 2017.

At P.S. 31, Samuel DuPont Elementary in Brooklyn, NY, the fourth-grade teacher engaged students in a reciprocal teaching lesson. Students worked in groups of four, where each student played a specific role: Questioner, Summarizer, Clarifier, or Predictor. Each student had to play his or her role in the group discussion about *the story they read. As students played their roles, they were required to cite evidence from the text in support of their conclusions. The teacher circulated to ensure that every student actively participated. In a short amount of time, each group had progressed into deep conversations about the story. Every student, including students with emerging bilingualism and students with disabilities, participated in conversations about character motives, word meanings, and plot development.*

> *P.S. 31, Samuel F. Dupont Elementary School is in Brooklyn, New York, in the New York City Department of Education's District 14. The school serves 600 students in prekindergarten through grade five. The school is a winner of the 2017 America's Best Urban Schools Award.*

Colorful pictures and neatly printed words covered the walls of classrooms in this inner-city Los Angeles school in the Montebello Unified School District. Barren wall spaces were rare, as students had literally thousands of reminders of the words they had learned throughout the year in various subject areas. In one first-grade classroom, the teacher pointed to a picture on the wall and asked, "Maria, what is this?"

"It is a picture of snow," Maria correctly answered.

"Yes, and what do we know about snow, Miguel?"

"Cold?" Miguel shyly answered, as if he hoped he had pulled the correct word from his small English vocabulary.

"In a complete sentence, please," insisted the teacher.

"Snow is cold. Snow is very cold," Miguel responded with a little more confidence.

"Excellent! And what else do you know about snow, Javier?"

"Snow falls from the sky in snowflakes."

"That's right! Snow falls from the sky in snowflakes. In summer?" the teacher challenged, pointing at Eva.

"No," Eva giggled and explained, "snow falls from the sky in winter."

"Are you sure about that, Manuel? I don't remember seeing any snow here in Los Angeles this winter," the teacher challenged again.

"Not here. In the mountains," Manuel explained.

"In a sentence," the teacher reminded.

"It doesn't snow here in Los Angeles. It snows in the mountains in winter."

Montebello Gardens Elementary School is in the Montebello Unified School District in Los Angeles, California. The school serves three hundred students in grades kindergarten through four. The school won the America's Best Urban School Award in 2009.

A Perpetual Question

On the Minds of Educators Striving to Produce Equity and Excellence

How can I get each and every one of my students to believe, "My teacher wants to help me be able to talk about and write about this topic as if I have been talking and writing about it all my life"?

In high-performing urban schools, teachers help students develop fluency with the vocabulary that serves as a gatekeeper to understanding challenging academic content. The gates of understanding swing open when students are fluent users of essential vocabulary related to the objective teachers want students to learn. Conversely, the gates of understanding remain closed when students cannot converse using key words and concepts. Students reach a deep level of understanding only when they have integrated key lesson vocabulary into their personal vocabularies.

Marzano and Pickering explained, "If students do not believe they can perform voluntary or required tasks relative to the information, the brain will eventually reject it" (2011, p. 19). If students perceive that they cannot talk about the concept; if they don't understand enough to be able to describe it, discuss it, or ask questions about it; or if they don't believe they can even read or pronounce the word, their brain is more likely to reject the information, and they will not achieve understanding and mastery.

In every subject area (including mathematics, science, English, social studies), students are likely to achieve understanding and mastery only when they have achieved fluency with the vocabulary most pertinent to the lesson. By developing the students' fluency with gatekeeper vocabulary, teachers build students' sense of efficacy related to the academic content. Students feel valued and capable when teachers have helped them become comfortable using academic language to discuss challenging concepts. As illustrated in Figure 6.1, building fluency with gatekeeper vocabulary contributes to a focus on understanding and mastery and contributes to students perceiving that they are valued and capable. Building fluency helps promote clarity by building students' capacity to share their understanding of lesson goals and success criteria. Building fluency helps ensure culturally, socially, and personally responsive teaching by helping teachers determine the extent to which students have integrated lesson concepts into the world they know and understand. As well, building fluency provides an excellent avenue for checking understanding and providing feedback.

In the science lesson described at the beginning of Chapter 2, the teacher at Horace Mann Dual Language Academy worked to ensure that every student was comfortable with the Spanish words for *volcano*, *magma*, *eruption*, and *pressure*. She checked in various ways to ensure that students were comfortable speaking and using these words in proper context. She wanted to know that her students could accurately explain the relationships between the concepts.

The middle school teacher at Rose Park Math and Science Magnet School was not content to see students listening quietly to his explanation of DNA extraction (in the lesson described at the beginning of this chapter). He wanted to hear his students explain key concepts and processes.

The third-grade teacher from Lyons Elementary in Houston was not satisfied that students could solve 54 times 3. Just as importantly, she wanted students to demonstrate that they could explain the algorithm and discuss why the algorithm made sense.

The fourth-grade teacher at Samuel Dupont in Brooklyn expected to see every student involved in asking questions, summarizing, clarifying, and predicting related to the novel the class was reading. Every student had to interact with the vocabulary and play a role in the group's success.

The first-grade teacher at Montebello Elementary in Los Angeles was not merely interested in having her students know the word "snow." She wanted to hear evidence that the students could talk about snow, comfortably and confidently. In each of these situations and hundreds more we observed in other high-performing urban schools, teachers deliberately endeavored to build student fluency with key lesson vocabulary.

Pre-Identifying Gatekeeper Vocabulary

In many of the lessons we observed in high-performing urban schools, teachers had pre-identified gatekeeper vocabulary words associated with each lesson. In particular, they focused upon words that conveyed important concepts, functions, and relationships associated with the lesson objective they wanted students to master.

Teachers at Signal Hill Elementary in Long Beach, California, carefully pre-identified important vocabulary words associated with the lessons they intended to teach. The teachers explained that this was essential to ensure the academic success of the many students with emerging bilingualism who attended their school. The teachers explained, "Many students who speak English at home have never or rarely heard some of the academic vocabulary that is important in our lessons. These words may be just as foreign to them as they are to our English learners."

Often, in high-performing urban schools, teachers worked together with their grade-level or department colleagues to identify lesson vocabulary that was likely to influence student understanding. For example, at Lauderbach, Montgomery, Otay, and Finney Elementary Schools in Chula Vista, California, teachers met in grade-level teams to determine how they would ensure that all students learned the challenging academic objectives they planned to teach. During these meetings, teachers asked themselves, "What words will our students need to know and understand in order to understand this concept well?" In such a meeting at Lauderbach, a primary-grade teacher explained to her colleagues that students needed to know the word "parallel" in order to accomplish their learning objective: distinguishing various two-dimensional shapes. The teacher correctly noted that students would not be able to articulate why some four-sided shapes were rectangles and others were not if they did not understand the concept of parallelism. The critical vocabulary words were recorded in planning team minutes, and lessons were designed to ensure that students learn those words.

By pre-identifying key vocabulary, teachers planned deliberately in ways that helped prevent unfamiliar vocabulary from barring their students from understanding the concepts central to their lesson objective. By thinking ahead about gatekeeper vocabulary, teachers were able to plan lessons so students were more likely to develop fluency with and feel efficacious regarding challenging concepts and skills.

Making New Vocabulary Seem Familiar

Krashen (1993) noted that vocabulary instruction in many classrooms is ineffective. Common strategies that require students to find and write dictionary definitions of words and write the words in sentences are often utilized as filler activities that fail to produce greater understanding and academic success. In contrast, in many high-performing urban schools, we saw teachers introducing new vocabulary in ways designed to make new words seem familiar to their students.

Figure 6.1

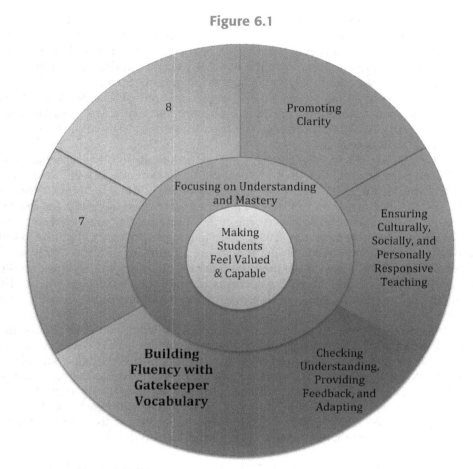

Specifically, in a manner consistent with the concepts discussed in Chapter 4, teachers presented new vocabulary in ways that helped students see the connections between the new vocabulary and their cultural, social, and/or personal backgrounds. For example, in a ninth-grade algebra lesson at MacArthur High School in Houston, Texas (Aldine Independent School District), a teacher had written the words *intercept* and *slope* on cards and placed them prominently on the board at the beginning of the lesson. She engaged students in describing common usages of the terms. Students responded by discussing interceptions in football or soccer. They also discussed the notion of mountain slopes. Next, the teacher pushed students to discuss how these common usages might apply to mathematics and to their specific lesson on graphing linear equations. Through these conversations, she helped students gain familiarity with the terms. They were better prepared to participate in instruction that required them to use these concepts.

In many of the classrooms we visited, we saw teachers introduce new vocabulary by helping students see connections with the concept in their native language.

For example, when Westcliff Elementary students in the Fort Worth Independent School District came upon the word "amiable" as they read a novel, the teacher was prepared. She had written the word on a card and shared it with her students. The students struggled to pronounce the word and could not determine the meaning. Then the teacher asked, "Do you know any words in Spanish that start with 'ami'?" Immediately, students answered "amigo" and "amiga." Without additional prompting, students made the connection. One student explained, "So, 'amiable' must mean 'friendly.' The character was a friendly person." The teacher made the new word instantly familiar.

In other classrooms, we saw teachers engaging students in physical actions that helped them become familiar with new vocabulary. For example, in a violin lesson at KIPP Adelante Academy in San Diego, California, the middle school music teacher asked, "What does *adagio* mean?" When a student answered correctly, the teacher exclaimed, "Yes, that's right! So what is *allegro*?" When a student answered correctly, the teacher played short measures on the violin and after each musical phrase asked, "So what is the tempo of that?" Students answered in unison with the words *adagio* or *allegro*. Then, the teacher asked students, "Play this line adagio. Play this line allegro," and students demonstrated the concepts through the use of their violins. The teacher made sure that students had a working understanding of these words prior to proceeding with the lesson.

Also at KIPP Adelante Academy, a science teacher led students in a game that required students to memorize hand signals for vocabulary words associated with a lesson on weather. Students worked in groups to practice the hand signals for *condensation, hurricane, evaporation, tornado*, and a few other words. The hand signals provided clues about the meaning of each word. The game engaged students in hearing, saying, and making hand movements associated with each word. By the time the game ended, students were well prepared to discuss the weather-related concepts in greater depth, because they were familiar with the vocabulary.

Building Fluency With and "Ownership" of Critical Vocabulary

In high-performing urban schools, teachers helped students acquire fluency with new vocabulary by motivating students to use the new vocabulary in oral and written communication they produced. Students were asked to discuss, explain, dramatize, describe, and debate in ways that gave them abundant opportunities to practice pronouncing and communicating with gatekeeper vocabulary.

Arechiga (2012) emphasized the importance of getting students to talk and practice using new vocabulary. Herrell and Jordan (2016) described several strategies that have proven effective in helping students with emerging bilingualism develop fluency with new vocabulary. In particular, they emphasized how interactive read-aloud strategies (such as encouraging students to describe orally personal experiences related to a text, explore alternate ways of saying things, or participate in the performance of a scene) can enhance students' understanding of new concepts. Additionally, they described how vocabulary role-play activities (in which groups of students are asked to write and perform skits in which new words are used and demonstrated) provide effective and motivating opportunities for practice. We observed these and other strategies being utilized in high-performing urban schools as teachers endeavored to build their students' fluency with and ownership of new vocabulary.

In the first-grade classroom at Montebello Gardens (discussed at the beginning of this chapter), the teacher made sure that her students did more than see or read the vocabulary. She made sure that students *owned* the vocabulary. By asking many questions and requiring students to answer in original sentences that utilized the central vocabulary, the teacher promoted student fluency and confidence. This teacher, like many teachers in high-performing schools, listened attentively and provided useful feedback to help students use the vocabulary accurately.

The teacher had already explained the term, but he wanted students to explain the term in their own words. Next, he asked them to identify liquids that were more or less viscous and explain why. The activity required students to speak the key vocabulary word multiple times with appropriate meaning. As the teacher circulated throughout the room, he prompted students to use the vocabulary even more. "Yes," he affirmed to one group of students and then asked, "So, what does that mean about honey?" A student responded, "Honey is more viscous than water." By the time the activity ended, almost every student had several opportunities to practice using the new vocabulary in the proper context.

At MC² STEM High School in Cleveland, Ohio, a teacher introduced the terms *compression* and *tension* as they relate to bridge engineering. The teacher demonstrated how compression points worked as students began to build their own bridges. As the teacher moved among the groups of students, he asked them to explain their designs in terms of compression points, tension, and other vocabulary terms related to bridge engineering. Students were given opportunities to practice the vocabulary the teacher wanted them to understand within the context of their design and construction projects.

In some schools, we observed teachers using sentence frames or paragraph frames to help students become more confident in using gatekeeper vocabulary. For example, at Bonham Elementary in the Dallas (Texas) Independent School District, a third-grade teacher engaged small groups of students in generating answers to the sentence frame, "I inferred that the main character was _____ because _____." Students were required to use the word *inferred*, but the sentence frame helped them do so accurately. Every student in the class used the word *infer* (in its various forms) multiple times during the lesson. The activity led students to understand and utilize the concept of inferences at a level that often eludes much older students. In contrast, in more typical schools, many students will experience lessons focused on inferences without ever uttering the words "infer" or "inference." In those cases, teachers might be inaccurately inferring that students will understand what is required of them when they are asked to make an inference.

At Columbus Elementary in Glendale, California, instructional aides were trained to help small groups of students learn and practice critical vocabulary words. In one classroom, while the teacher worked with a group of students on a guided reading activity, the instructional aide helped a different group practice key vocabulary words. The aide reminded the students about the meaning of a word and challenged students to engage in dialogue, using the word frequently.

For example, an aide presented the word *astonished* and then asked students, "How would you feel if a kid brought an elephant to school?" Students immediately answered that they would be astonished, so the aide asked, "Why would you be astonished?" Each student in the group answered the question, using the vocabulary word correctly. The aide continued to guide the conversation so that students were encouraged to use the word "astonished" many times.

Muhammad and Hollie (2012) described the reciprocal teaching strategy used at Samuel Dupont Elementary in Brooklyn. Through this strategy, each student assumed an important role (summarizing, clarifying, questioning, or predicting) in the group's dialogue about the text. Also, Muhammad and Hollie described the use of reader's theater as a strategy for providing students opportunities to develop fluency with key vocabulary and concepts. At Fay Herron Elementary in Las Vegas, Nevada, we observed a primary class presenting a reader's theater version of *The Cat in the Hat*. In front of a large audience of parents, the students performed enthusiastically, in a manner that suggested they would always remember the vocabulary of the story.

In many high-performing urban schools, teachers engaged students in writing as a strategy for building fluency with new vocabulary. Krashen explained, "When we write our ideas down, the vague and abstract become clear and concrete" (1993, p. 76). In all curricular areas, students were expected to write in ways that explained their understanding of important ideas and concepts. In many schools, teachers expected students to practice new vocabulary in writing activities. As students became more familiar with vocabulary, teachers required students to write paragraphs, letters, stories, and essays in which they utilized the key vocabulary in original sentences. For example, at Golden Empire Elementary in Sacramento, California, we saw student writing assignments that explained the distinctions between animal classifications. At Charles Lunsford Elementary in Rochester, New York, we saw student writing samples that explained the procedure for solving multistep math problems. At Hambrick Middle School in Houston, Texas, students wrote explanations for the different roles and responsibilities of the three branches of the federal government. In all of these and many other examples, writing activities gave students the opportunity to practice using the vocabulary they had discussed during the lesson.

It is important to note that strategies for promoting students' fluency with gatekeeper vocabulary will not work in an atmosphere where students fear making errors with language. Students will creatively avoid speaking or writing if they perceive that doing so is likely to result in their embarrassment or humiliation.

In the high-performing schools we studied, teachers worked hard to help students know they would not be teased, embarrassed, or ridiculed by the teacher or by other students. When students made errors, teachers or other students provided gentle correction but also congratulated students for demonstrating courage. As well, teachers reminded students that their small errors were positive steps toward learning and exceling. Students became comfortable taking risks because they knew teachers would ensure their emotional safety.

Sustaining Fluency

To promote the continued use of important vocabulary words, many teachers in high-performing urban schools implemented strategies to help ensure that students would maintain fluency with gatekeeper vocabulary. Two of the most frequently used strategies were word walls and personal glossaries.

In many classrooms in high-performing urban schools, teachers prominently posted the vocabulary words students had learned. These word walls were referred to often throughout lessons. Teachers often acknowledged students for using posted vocabulary correctly. In many classrooms, like the first-grade classroom at Montebello, word walls became giant glossaries that helped students remember and practice the words they had learned. The word walls were also valuable tools for improving student writing.

Word walls were not just static room decorations. Instead, they were dynamic instructional tools utilized by teachers and students as an ever-present prompt for remembering and utilizing important lesson vocabulary. At the same time, word walls were often implicit celebrations of the vocabulary students had learned. At MacArthur High, important vocabulary words were hung in each corridor as reminders of the concepts students had learned.

Additionally, in many of the classrooms we visited, teachers engaged students in creating, maintaining, and using personal glossaries or dictionaries. As new words were introduced, studied, and discussed, students were expected to maintain their personal collection of new vocabulary words. In some classrooms, the glossaries were compiled in spiral-bound notebooks. Other teachers punched holes in a corner of 3 × 5 cards, and students kept an ever-growing collection of cards upon which they wrote definitions, drew illustrations, wrote the word in their first language, and provided themselves other hints for remembering the word, the word's meaning, and the appropriate uses of the word.

In many classes, students placed their personal glossaries on their desks when they started writing activities. During classroom conversations, students would look for a word in their personal glossary or find the word on the classroom word wall. These tools helped students continue to "own" the new words they had learned.

Summary

In high-performing urban schools, students were more likely to achieve understanding and mastery, in part because their teachers helped them develop and maintain fluency with key lesson vocabulary. Teachers did not assume that students would acquire fluency simply by hearing the teacher speak the word or the definition, looking up the word in the dictionary, or engaging in other busywork related to the new word. Instead, teachers understood that fluency would be developed only when students had many opportunities to practice speaking and writing the new vocabulary.

To build students' fluency, teachers deliberately pre-identified gatekeeper vocabulary associated with the lessons they taught. Teachers worked with their colleagues to identify which words were key to students' ability to understand challenging concepts. Teachers introduced these new words in ways that quickly made them seem familiar. By responding to students' cultural, social, and personal backgrounds, teachers were able to help students draw important connections. Additionally, teachers provided many rich opportunities for students to practice using gatekeeper vocabulary orally and in writing. By utilizing the new words frequently, students were able to integrate the new vocabulary into their everyday vocabulary. Finally, teachers provided students easy ways to capture, remember, and refer to the vocabulary they had practiced and learned.

What It Is & What It Isn't

Building Fluency with Gatekeeper Vocabulary

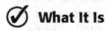 What It Is

Pre-identifying the vocabulary students must learn in order to achieve the lesson objective

> Example: A statistics teacher considers the vocabulary students need to master in order to have a deep understanding of the concept of standard deviation. The teacher identifies a list of critical terms, including some that students should have already learned (e.g., mean, median, data set) and some new words (e.g., frequency, standard, deviation, normal curve, distribution). The teacher plans a lesson to ensure that students have multiple opportunities to demonstrate that they understand these words before she introduces the concept of standard deviation.

⊗ What It Isn't

Starting a lesson without considering which vocabulary words might become stumbling blocks that impede mastery

> Example: A statistics teacher introduces a lesson on standard deviation. The teacher wants students to understand and be able to use the concept of standard deviation. The teacher methodically shares with students the procedure for calculating the standard deviation of a data set. To help make the lesson interesting, the teacher uses data sets that are familiar to the students. Learning, however, is limited because students are not conversant with several of the terms the teacher uses, including *distribution*, *deviation*, and *frequency*.

✓ What It Is

Making new vocabulary seem familiar

> Example: An alternative high school teacher is endeavoring to get his class to understand the concept of "hesitation" because a key aspect of the climax of the novel they are reading is the wolf's hesitation before racing away from the hunter. As the teacher anticipated, the students could not pronounce the word "hesitation" accurately and were not certain of the meaning. "How many of you like basketball?" the teacher asked. Instantly, there seemed to be more raised hands than there were students in the room. What does the term "hesitation dribble" mean in basketball? A few of the students responded accurately that a hesitation dribble was a basketball technique in which a player with the ball slows momentarily and then bursts past the opponent at full speed. "So,

why does a player use a hesitation dribble?" the teacher asked. A student explained, "It's a way of faking out your opponent." Then another added, "Yeah, you hesitate to make the other guy think you're going to stop, but then you blow right past him!" "Wait, I get it," another student chimes in. "The wolf was outsmarting the hunter. When the hunter slowed down, the wolf was going to zoom past him." "Let's keep reading to see," the teacher suggested.

⊗ What It Isn't

Introducing important new vocabulary in ways that are not likely to connect with students' cultural, social, or personal backgrounds

Example: An alternative high school teacher is endeavoring to get his students to understand the concept of "hesitation." He asks students to find the word in the dictionary, copy the definition, and write an original sentence with the word. When the students approached the word in the story, most students still could not pronounce the word, and they were uncertain about the meaning, in part because the dictionary definition referred to an act of hesitating and included unfamiliar words like "faltering." Other students were uncertain because, in their minds, it seemed illogical for the wolf to pause or hesitate, considering the hunter's proximity.

⊘ What It Is

Building fluency with and "ownership" of critical vocabulary

Example: The teacher shared with students a handcrafted, felt board model of an animal cell and explained that the students would learn about the various parts of the cell, their names, and their functions. The teacher removed a few felt pieces from the board and explained, "These are mitochondria. Everyone say 'mitochondria.'" The teacher explained why mitochondria are important to the cell. Then she handed the felt pieces to a student and asks, "What are you holding?" When the student answered "mitochondria," the teacher asked about their function. The teacher invited the student to give the mitochondria to another student and explain what he or she was giving. The teacher then asked the second student similar questions about the mitochondria. Then the teacher asked all the students what would happen to the animal if all of the mitochondria were removed. Students worked in pairs to generate a complete answer with strong rationale. Then the teacher called upon several students to share their responses before she moved to the next organelle on the felt board. By the lesson's end, every student had pronounced the key vocabulary multiple times. As well, they had spoken sentences to the teacher and their classmates explaining the function of each cell component.

(X) What It Isn't

Engaging students in routine vocabulary activities that do not require students to use new vocabulary frequently

Example: In a lesson on the structure of animal cells, the teacher has students use the glossary of their biology text to find the definitions of several components of animal cells. Students must write the definitions on worksheets and create posters showing an animal cell with the appropriately labeled parts.

(✓) What It Is

Engaging students in writing original text to practice the use of new vocabulary

Example: As an opening activity for each class, a government teacher requires students to write a paragraph concerning a concept discussed in the previous day's lesson. Each writing prompt asks students to write about a problem or an issue associated with the main vocabulary concept introduced. For example, after a lesson on bicameral legislatures, an opening activity requires students to write a paragraph that explains why bicameral legislative governments might generate gridlock.

(X) What It Isn't

Engaging students in copying words or sentences that use new vocabulary

Example: A government teacher requires students to copy a set of words that relate to the day's lesson on the legislative branch of government. Students must also copy a set of sentences that correspond to each vocabulary word. Students keep the words and sentences in their government class journals.

(✓) What It Is

Building and maintaining students' trust that they will not be humiliated when they make language errors

Example: In response to a teacher's question about sequencing events, a student explained, "I sequence events in the story to tell how things are alike and how they are different." The teacher responded, "That is a great answer to explain comparing and contrasting. Sequencing, however, has something to do with the order of things. Do you recall what sequencing means?" Quickly, the student responds, "Oh yes, I got my words mixed up. Sequencing is about putting things in the order they happened." "Excellent answer!" the teacher affirms.

⊗ What It Isn't

Making students feel embarrassed when they answer incorrectly

Example: Example: In response to a teachers question about sequencing events, a student explained, "I sequence events in the story to tell how things are alike and how they are different." The teacher responded, "Wrong," in a neutral voice, but rolled her eyes in a manner obvious to all students in the classroom, as if she were saying, "Where did he get that wild answer?"

⊘ What It Is

Sustaining fluency

Example: A third-grade teacher maintains a word wall that includes vocabulary from each story the class has read. The word wall is divided into five large sections: nouns, verbs, adjectives, adverbs, and other parts of speech. When a new story is introduced, students engage in discussions of the selected vocabulary words. Students must place the word in the correct word-wall section in alphabetical order. Working in teams, students develop "model sentences" that reflect various uses of each vocabulary word. A few of the model sentences get posted next to the appropriate vocabulary word on the word wall. Students receive bonus points when they use any word-wall words in their writing assignments if the words are used in an appropriate context and spelled correctly. At the end of each reading lesson, the teacher engages students in a random review of one word from each section of the word wall.

⊗ What It Isn't

Having word walls as wall coverings

Example: A third-grade reading teacher maintains a word wall that includes vocabulary from each story the class has read. Before a story is read, the teacher posts five or six vocabulary words on the word wall. When the story is introduced, the teacher carefully discusses each of the vocabulary words and engages students in discussion of the words. After the initial discussion of the new vocabulary, the teacher does not refer to the word wall or encourage its use.

Practice Guide Related to Building Fluency With Gatekeeper Vocabulary

For information on possible uses of this practice guide, please see page xiii in the Preface.

1. In the lesson observed, what vocabulary might be considered gate-keeper vocabulary? List the words and concepts most likely to influence whether students would achieve the objective of the lesson observed. Then rank each of the vocabulary words/concepts in order of importance to achieving the lesson objective (i.e., 1 is highest importance, 2 is next highest, etc.).

    • _____

    • _____

    • _____

    • _____

2. What did you observe that suggested that the teacher had pre-identified and prepared to teach students the gatekeeper vocabulary?

    _____

    _____

3. For the gatekeeper word ranked most important, what did the teacher do to introduce the concept to students?

    _____

    _____

4. For the gatekeeper word ranked second most important, what did the teacher do to introduce the concept to students?

    _____

    _____

5. Did any of the strategies used for introducing gatekeeper vocabulary connect with the students' cultural, social, or personal backgrounds? _____ If yes, which students or groups of students were likely to perceive a connection? _____

    What did the teacher do to help students make a connection with gatekeeper words?

    _____

    _____

6. To help answer the next group of items, create a simple map of the classroom. In particular, include all of the desks where students sit. Make circles on the map to represent where each student sits. Make a tally mark in each student's circle when you hear the student using one of the gatekeeper vocabulary words you identified as most important. When the lesson ends, look at your map. Do you notice any patterns? Are any students or groups of students more likely or less likely to have acquired fluency with gatekeeper vocabulary?

7. Which strategies did the teacher utilize to help students develop fluency with and ownership of the gatekeeper vocabulary?

   • Read-aloud activities that required students to relate concepts, explain ideas, and use gatekeeper vocabulary

   • Vocabulary role-play activities that required students to write and act out skits that explained gatekeeper vocabulary

   • Teacher-to-student oral questions that engaged all students in discussing gatekeeper vocabulary

   • Partner talk that required students to discuss gatekeeper vocabulary with a peer

   • Use of sentence frames and paragraph frames to promote the use of gatekeeper vocabulary

   • Small-group discussions designed to engage students in using gatekeeper vocabulary

   • Reciprocal teaching that highlights gatekeeper vocabulary

   • Reader's theater that engages all students in using gatekeeper vocabulary

   • Original, purposeful writing that engages students in writing, using gatekeeper vocabulary

   • Other _____

8. Did the strategies utilized engage all, most, or few students in practicing the gatekeeper vocabulary? _____ Which strategies were most effective in engaging which students or student groups?

   _____

   _____

9. From the strategies listed in item 7, which strategies might the teacher employ to increase the extent to which students develop fluency with gatekeeper vocabulary?

   _____

   _____

10. What strategies were employed in the classroom to help sustain students' fluency with gatekeeper vocabulary?

_____

_____

Practical Next Steps ☀

1. In collaboration with teacher colleagues, engage in a book study of Chapter 10 of *The Will to Lead, the Skill to Teach: Transforming Schools at Every Level* (Muhammad & Hollie, 2012). While this chapter provides many excellent strategies for improving culturally, socially, and personally responsive teaching, several of the strategies are particularly helpful for helping students use, practice, and develop fluency with new vocabulary.

2. In collaboration with colleagues, plan your teaching of the next important student-learning goal with special attention to gatekeeper vocabulary. Ask yourselves, "What are the words/concepts students will need to know well in order to have a high likelihood of achieving the learning goal?" Design strategies to (a) introduce the new vocabulary in ways that are likely to connect with your students' backgrounds, (b) provide your students with abundant opportunities to practice using the gatekeeper vocabulary and develop fluency, and (c) provide your students with supports that will help them sustain their understanding of the gatekeeper vocabulary.

3. Using your class roster, identify the third of your students who are probably the least likely to "own" the gatekeeper vocabulary of the next lesson you plan to teach. Write their names on a sheet of paper that you attach to a clipboard. During the lesson, deliberately endeavor to ensure each student listed on the clipboard uses the gatekeeper vocabulary in a meaningful sentence. Be patient, supportive, and positive, helping the students know that you are truly invested in their success. Place a check by each student's name when you see or hear evidence that the student tried to utilize the gatekeeper vocabulary. Place a star by the student's name when you feel confident that the student is comfortable using the gatekeeper vocabulary.

References

Arechiga, D. (2012). *Reaching English language learners in every classroom: Energizers for teaching and learning*. Larchmont, NY: Eye On Education.

Herrell, A. L., & Jordan, M. (2016). *50 strategies for teaching English language learners* (5th ed.). Boston: Pearson.

Krashen, S. D. (1993). *The power of reading: Insights from the research*. Westport, CT: Libraries Unlimited.

Marzano, R. J., & Pickering, D. J. (2011). *The highly engaged classroom*. Bloomington, IN: Marzano Research Laboratory.

Muhammad, A., & Hollie, S. (2012). *The will to lead and the skill to teach: Transforming schools at every level*. Bloomington, IN: Solution Tree.

Promoting Successful Practice

In a third-grade classroom at Horace Mann Elementary School in Glendale, California, the objective read, "Today, I will learn to order numbers." The teacher read the objective and asked, "What does it mean to order numbers?"

"It means to put them in order," offered one child.

"What if someone doesn't know what 'order' means? How would you explain what it means to order numbers?"

Another student suggested, "It means to put the smallest first, then the next bigger one, then the next, until you're done."

"Yes," the teacher affirmed. "That's one meaning. Putting numbers in order can mean placing them from least to greatest. Is there another way of putting them in order?"

"Well, you could switch them from greatest to least," proposed another student.

"Absolutely! That's another way of ordering numbers, from greatest to least. Today, you're going to show me that you can order numbers from least to greatest and from greatest to least. First, I need someone to remind us what least means?"

"It means the smallest," answered a student.

"That's right. And, what does greatest mean?" queried the teacher.

"It means the biggest," answered another child.

The teacher quickly reminded students about a strategy for comparing the size of three-digit numbers. She demonstrated the strategy with the help of a document camera.

"Look. I have these three numbers: 329, 347, and 315. I need to put them in order from the greatest to the least. Let's see. Where should I start?"

"With the hundreds place?" offered one student.

"Why would I start there?" asked the teacher.

"Because you want to find which one is biggest, so you need to start with the biggest place value."

"Yes. That makes sense," the teacher affirmed as she underlined the numeral in the hundred's place in all three numbers. "But that didn't help me much because all of the numbers have a three in the hundreds place."

"So, go to the tens place," suggested another student.

"Why?" asked the teacher, looking as if she really needed help understanding.

"Because it's the next-biggest place value after the hundreds," answered a student.

"OK," the teacher sighed, "but are you sure this is going to help me figure out which number is greatest?"

Students eagerly offered explanations for why the strategy would help identify the largest number.

The teacher continued to model the strategy while asking students questions at each step. Finally, she had the three numbers placed in the proper sequence, and every student had participated in answering at least one question about the process.

"Now, I want you to work with your partner and show me that you know how to order these three numbers from greatest to least." The teacher projected three three-digit numerals through the document camera. Students worked in pairs and recorded their answers on individual white boards. While the students worked, the teacher quickly circulated around the room, determining which students understood and which ones did not.

After a few minutes, the teacher asked everyone to display their answers. Almost all of the pairs answered correctly. She asked students (including those who answered incorrectly) to explain why the correct answer was accurate. One student who answered incorrectly on his white board explained the rationale for the correct answer and explained how he and his partner made an error in the process.

The teacher repeated the process by asking students to order three more three-digit numbers. This time, however, she specified that she wanted students to sequence them from least to greatest. "What are you going to do differently this time?" she asked.

"We've got to find the smallest and put it first," responded a student.

"That's right!" the teacher affirmed and encouraged students to proceed in pairs again, writing their answers on their white boards.

This time, all of the students answered correctly. Again, she asked students to explain their responses. Then she asked students to practice individually by ordering two sets of three numbers from least to greatest and ordering two sets of three numbers from greatest to least. While students worked individually, the teacher continued to circulate and monitor each child's progress.

Horace Mann Elementary is in the Glendale Unified School District in Glendale, California. The school serves approximately 720 students in grades kindergarten through five. The school won the America's Best Urban Schools Award in 2010 and 2016.

A Perpetual Question

On the Minds of Educators Striving to Produce Equity and Excellence

How can I get each and every one of my students to believe, "I can accomplish whatever challenging tasks my teacher assigns (if I work hard) because my teacher carefully guides me so I am prepared to succeed"?

Hattie (2009) reported that well-planned practice had a substantial effect on student learning results. He emphasized that practice was most effective when teachers were able to increase the rate of correct academic responses until mastery was achieved. He stressed that this type of practice was not dull and repetitive drill. Instead, the findings pointed to the importance of aiming toward deeper and conceptual understandings.

Not all practice is productive. In fact, practice can be counterproductive if it occurs in a manner that allows the student to repeat errors until inaccurate thinking hardens like concrete, resistant to the penetration of more precise information or strategies. Also, practice can be counter-productive if it results in students deciding that the content is boring, meaningless, or beyond their ability to comprehend.

In high-performing urban schools, teachers ensure that students have at least a moderate understanding of a concept before they ask students to perform the task independently. Generally, students are not asked to practice concepts or skills they do not understand well. In more typical schools, students are often pushed to work independently on tasks that they are ill prepared to pursue. As a result, in more typical schools, students often spend hours practicing incorrect strategies, algorithms, and processes. Misunderstandings, after they have been practiced to perfection, are difficult to correct.

By promoting successful practice, teachers help ensure that students achieve learning goals. As illustrated in Figure 7.1, promoting successful practice helps ensure that all of the other teaching practices work together in a way that results in understanding and mastery. As well, when teachers promote successful practice, students are much more likely to feel valued and capable. They experience confirmation of their ability through their everyday academic conversations, their success solving academic problems, and their everyday assignments. Through successful practice, students feel efficacious about learning and become ready to take on the next learning task.

Figure 7.1

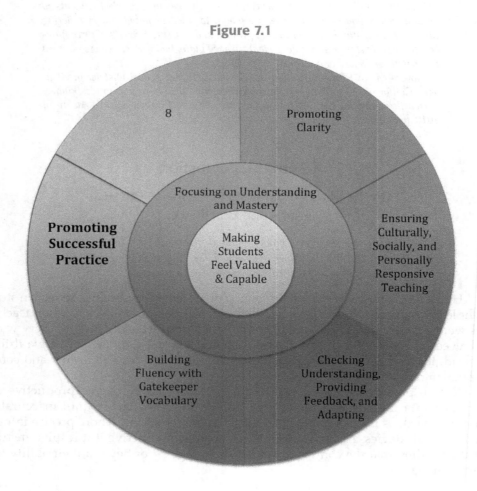

Guiding Students Toward Independent Learning

In a struggling urban high school, we observed that most lessons were organized in a consistent pattern. Each class period began with a "Do Now" activity, intended to allow students to practice previously learned skills for a few minutes while the teacher took attendance and collected homework. Typically, however, the "Do Now" took 15 or 20 minutes. Then the teacher spent another 5 to 10 minutes correcting the "Do Now." Often, the teacher asked the students, "What is the answer for question one? What was your answer for question two?" As students answered and the teacher affirmed or corrected their responses, all students were supposed to check their work. Usually, more than half the class answered fewer than half of the "Do Now" items correctly. Then, with almost half of the class period elapsed, the teacher would state the day's lesson objective or have a student read the objective, and the teacher would spend 10 to 15 minutes "teaching" the new objective with little or no checking to determine if students understood the concepts being taught. Then, almost ritualistically, the teacher would begin passing out worksheets while saying, "Here's your assignment. You are to work on this without talking. Whatever you do not finish is your homework. Bring this back finished tomorrow. Any questions?" Customarily, less than half of the students understood sufficiently to answer the worksheets correctly. Some students did not attempt to complete the assignments, providing additional evidence for the teachers who believed that student apathy was the primary reason the school's test scores were dismal.

In this struggling school, teachers acted as if they assumed that their students were prepared to pursue academic tasks independently after only a few minutes of lecture. Educators (including the school administrators) tended to assume that teaching consisted of presenting new information and assigning independent work. When asked to explain their rationale for this approach, school leaders claimed, "This is research based." Teachers claimed, "We need to have a grade in the grade book for each student, each day they are in attendance. This gives us a way to prove that we are teaching." Unfortunately, there are many urban classrooms where this routine is commonplace.

In stark contrast, in high-performing urban schools, teachers design lessons to maximize the likelihood that every student achieves the learning goal. Just as a potter would not place a bowl in the kiln until it was perfectly shaped, teachers do not place their students in independent learning situations until the teacher knows their students are ready and that the independent learning is likely to result in success for each student. In high-performing urban schools, teachers don't rush toward independent practice. They take time to help make sure students attend to the proper strategies, related nuances, and potential missteps. They want to know that each student understands how to pursue the task and why the process works before they release students to work independently. In the third-grade class from Horace Mann Elementary, described at the beginning of this chapter, the teacher was not satisfied to hear students offer the correct answer. She wanted to hear students explain why each step made sense. She wanted to ensure that students had a high likelihood of success before she allowed her students to work independently.

Fisher and Frey (2014) built upon the work of Pearson and Gallagher (1983) to develop a four-stage instructional framework for the gradual release of responsibility, including focused instruction, guided instruction, collaborative learning, and independent learning. In high-performing urban schools, we have observed hundreds of examples of teachers utilizing this framework to help students understand and master learning goals. The framework starts with focused instruction that helps students understand what they are learning, why they are learning, and how they will learn it. In focused learning, teachers establish the purpose for the lesson, model the learning behaviors students will be expected to emulate, and notice when students are ready for the next part of the framework: guided instruction. In guided instruction, teachers share information, strategies, and skills but also use many questions to determine the extent of student understanding. Through guided instruction, teachers seek to verify that each student knows how to proceed independently and understands why processes are likely to generate intended outcomes. Rosenshine (1983) found that students who benefitted from frequent checking for understanding during guided instruction were more likely to succeed at independent practice. In the gradual-release framework, the teacher assumes primary responsibility for both focused instruction and guided instruction.

When teachers are confident that students understand the essential concepts and processes associated with the lesson, teachers proceed to provide collaborative learning activities. Rosenshine (1983) found that cooperative learning activities could be powerful tools for helping students practice successfully. Collaborative learning offers students an opportunity to practice concepts and skills with the support of their peers. By working in small groups on tasks directly related to the learning goal, students are encouraged to work with and talk with each other to achieve a learning outcome. As a student at Magnet Traditional School in Phoenix, Arizona, explained, "We don't just learn from our teachers; we learn from our class. We have partner work and we work together."

During collaborative learning, teachers continuously observe, noting what students understand, what they don't understand, what they have learned, and what they still need to learn. Teachers carefully assess each student's readiness for the final stage of the framework: independent learning. Independent learning is structured to deepen students' learning through independent application and extension.

In high-performing elementary, middle, and high schools, we observed teachers meticulously preparing students to work independently with high rates of success. For example, at Louisa May Alcott Elementary in Cleveland, Ohio, primary-grade reading teachers modeled how students should decode words (focused instruction) and then provided every student multiple opportunities to decode the words in the story correctly (guided instruction) before they asked students to read the story in groups. At Franklin Towne Charter High School in Philadelphia, Pennsylvania, an algebra teacher gave every student in the classroom at least two opportunities to explain parts of the quadratic equation and answer questions about the equation's meaning (guided instruction) before she allowed students to open their textbooks and answer similar questions independently. At William Dandy Middle School in Fort Lauderdale, Florida, science teachers required students to use the graphic organizers they created in small groups to explain the concepts they had learned about genetics (collaborative learning). The teacher listened carefully as students explained their graphic organizers to each other. When the teacher was confident that students could explain orally, the teacher gave students a short quiz addressing the same concepts (independent learning). Marzano (2010) refers to examples such as these as "structured practice." He explained that the practice was structured to "maximize students' success rates" (p. 80).

Even when students seemed ready to proceed to work independently, teachers checked to make sure that all students understood key directions prior to allowing students to work independently. For example, a teacher at Dreamkeepers Academy in Norfolk, Virginia, asked her students, "What will you need to do in order to write this report? What will you have to do first?"

Quickly, she called upon a student who did not have his hand raised. "First, we have to complete the concept map," the student answered correctly.

"How are you going to do that?" the teacher asked, pointing to another child.

"We're going to get information about the different kinds of rock from our chapter and show it on the concept map?" the student answered and asked simultaneously.

The teacher continued to probe. She asked various students to explain what information they were going to collect, how they were going to display the information, and how they were going to use the concept map to organize their report. It quickly became obvious that students knew how to proceed in a manner that would allow them to complete the assignment successfully.

As a result of this kind of persistent checking, almost all students were able to proceed with minimal or no teacher assistance. Little or no time was wasted with students trying to figure out how they should begin or what they should do. While this type of checking took more time than simply asking, "Any questions?" teachers saved time that would have otherwise been spent repeating directions or redirecting off-task students.

While we observed hundreds of classrooms in which teachers used elements of the gradual-release-of-responsibility framework, the four stages of the framework did not necessarily comprise a rigidly followed ritual or routine. Teachers chose their next teaching move based on their observations of their students. Carefully, teachers sought to determine if each student was progressing toward readiness for independent learning. In some cases, guided instruction was followed by more focused instruction when teachers determined that students missed key lesson concepts. By observing their students, teachers determined what strategies they would use, how they would group students, how they would differentiate learning, and what questions they would ask to ensure that each student progressed to understanding and mastering the lesson objective independently.

Guiding Students to Learn Difficult Concepts

In high-performing urban schools we studied, students struggled to learn difficult concepts. Efforts to carefully guide students toward successful independent practice did not eliminate struggle. Instead, effective teaching practices increased the likelihood that struggle was fruitful for every student. In high-performing urban schools, students had to struggle as they sought to learn and apply concepts and skills that were at grade level and beyond. As the principal of Whitefoord Elementary in Atlanta, Georgia, explained:

> If all of the children are able to answer all of the questions, there is something wrong—they're not learning new information. I want to make sure the lesson is rigorous enough that some of the information [the teacher] is

giving is *new* information, and that [students] are making connections, but I'm concerned if they can answer every single thing and process and digest everything the teacher is giving.

In high-performing urban schools, teachers are masterful at guiding students through difficult concepts. Teachers ask questions, raise issues, and pose challenges that lead students from what they know to what they need to know in order to understand challenging concepts. Instruction of this caliber requires planning. At many high-performing urban schools, such as Highland Elementary in Silver Spring, Maryland, and Otay Elementary in Chula Vista, California, teachers work in teams to deliberately plan how they will guide students to understand difficult concepts. They plan what questions they will ask, and they anticipate the correct and incorrect answers students will provide. They consider how they will use both correct and incorrect answers to lead students to more complete understandings of the concepts they endeavor to teach.

Monitoring Independent Work

In high-performing urban schools, even when students are given independent work, teachers monitor carefully to ensure students are practicing successfully. Typically, we saw teachers looking over students' shoulders, inspecting their work, and checking to make sure students were answering correctly. Students were not allowed to practice repeatedly in an incorrect manner. For example, when a teacher determined that an individual student misunderstood an important aspect of the lesson, the teacher provided immediate assistance. When the teacher surmised that a few students were perplexed or confounded by the concept, the teacher immediately called together the struggling students and provided additional instruction, while other students continued to work independently. On the other hand, if all students were making significant errors, the teacher might abruptly stop the independent work and immediately revert to focused instruction, using the observed student errors as teaching tools.

Building Student Capacity to Self-Monitor

In high-performing urban schools, often, teachers equip students with strategies for checking their independent work or their work at learning centers. If students are provided with written directions, rubrics, scoring guides, or similar tools, they can self-assess and determine that they are "on target" as they pursue mastery. Students are more likely to maximize their effort when they know they are performing at a level that will earn a strong grade and ensure their mastery of the concept or skill. Simultaneously, students are more likely to ask for focused assistance when a rubric or scoring guide helps them determine that they have not learned a key concept or skill well.

At several high-performing schools, teachers made extensive use of rubrics to help students evaluate their work. For example, at Branch Brook Elementary in Newark, New Jersey, students knew precisely what they needed to do as they worked to "Strive for a 5" in the school's writing program. Throughout Maplewood Richmond Heights High School, teachers utilized and posted rubrics that articulated both what students were expected to learn and how students were expected to present what they had learned. Detailed rubrics helped students evaluate their work while they were writing. Students could self-correct in a timely manner. Also, students could use the rubrics to evaluate their writing when they completed assignments. In some classes, students took pride in predicting their scores because they understood the rubrics and used them well.

Providing Independent Practice (Including Homework) Worth Completing

Marzano (2010) emphasized that independent practice activities (including homework) should relate directly and explicitly to identified learning goals, should be calibrated to the right level of difficulty so students can complete assignments independently, and should be structured to ensure high completion rates. Independent practice should give students meaningful opportunities to practice concepts and skills they have learned. It should not be boring, meaningless repetition. Throughout our observations of high-performing urban schools, we did not see endless seatwork or thick packets of worksheets. Independent practice was focused upon the specific objective the teacher wanted students to master. Independent practice was long enough to confirm that students had truly acquired mastery, yet it was short enough and interesting enough to sustain a high level of student engagement.

In many high-performing urban schools, independent work was differentiated. Hill and Flynn (2006) emphasized that practice activities (including homework) should be differentiated to address students' needs, strengths, and language abilities. As well, they encouraged teachers to utilize concrete, nonlinguistic examples, including opportunities for students to ask questions and discuss assignments orally, receive native-language support, and receive modified or additional instruction. At Wildflower Elementary in Colorado Springs, Colorado, instruction was designed so that all students would achieve challenging state standards; however, assignments were sometimes differentiated to help students progress toward high levels of understanding and mastery. Tomlinson and Moon (2013) referred to this practice as "teaching up" (p. 8). Teachers planned tasks for students who were achieving at advanced levels and then differentiated by providing assignments that helped all students progress toward the advanced-level tasks. Similarly, at Westcliff Elementary in Fort Worth, Texas, teachers focused upon "differentiation for all" to help ensure every student would have challenging, independent learning experiences that helped advance their understanding and mastery of learning goals.

Teachers, parents, and students reported that homework was regularly assigned, completed, graded, and returned. Students perceived that homework provided them an opportunity to show how much they had learned. Neither students nor parents tended to perceive that homework was drudgery. Students in high-performing urban schools reported that they succeeded in completing homework regularly. "Yes, we get homework, but it's not too hard and not too easy. You don't have to be a genius to finish your homework," a student at Franklin Towne Charter High School in Philadelphia, Pennsylvania, explained. A parent at Golden Empire Elementary in Sacramento, California, described the differences between homework her child received at Golden Empire and homework the child had received at another school. She remarked:

> At the other school, my child got less homework, but it took him longer to do it. Often, I had to spend a lot of time teaching the math work he needed in order to do the assignment. Here [at Golden Empire], he gets more home- work, but he's able to finish it by himself with almost no help from me. Even the math, he's able to do pretty quickly by himself.

In these high-performing urban schools, students perceived their ability to complete homework as evidence that they were smart, talented, and capable. For example, at Lemay Elementary in Los Angeles, California, a child remarked, "The homework is pretty hard, but it's good that they are pushing us . . . we're learning a lot more."

Summary

Abraham Lincoln reportedly said, "Give me six hours to chop down a tree, and I will spend the first five sharpening the axe." In high-performing urban schools, much more time was devoted to guided instruction and collaborative learning than to either focused instruction or independent learning. Teachers devoted the nec- essary time to "sharpening the axe" through guided instruction and collaborative instruction. Students were allowed to practice independently (start chopping) only when the teacher had seen evidence that students possessed the knowledge and/or skill necessary to proceed successfully.

It is important to emphasize that teachers deliberately guided each and every student toward independent learning. The success of Black, Latino, Native Ameri- can, and Southeast Asian students, students with emerging bilingualism, students with disabilities, students experiencing homelessness, and many other students who have traditionally been underserved was ensured because teachers purposefully structured efforts to guide them to independent success. In the absence of deliber- ate efforts to guide students toward independent learning, it is unlikely that schools would have achieved such impressive outcomes for every demographic group of students.

The notion of promoting successful practice seems so logical. Why would edu- cators design instruction in any other way? Why is this difficult? Why are there so many schools like the struggling urban high school described earlier in this chapter where the prevailing strategy seemed designed to promote unsuccessful practice?

Many urban educators may believe they retain greater control of their class- rooms and their school when they minimize teacher–student interaction (as required in guided instruction) and eliminate student–student interaction (as required in cooperative learning) and maximize the time students spend completing routine tasks (busywork). Some teachers and administrators persist in their use of counter- productive practice strategies, in part because they worry that behavior problems would escalate if they abandoned their ineffective teaching routines.

Ironically, in the high-performing schools we visited, we found dramatically fewer behavior issues than were present in other struggling urban schools in the same neighborhoods. Students discovered learning was enjoyable and rewarding. Students recognized they were becoming capable scholars. Teachers learned their energies were better spent on working diligently to ensure each student would learn and experience academic success. We don't naively suggest that the transition from worksheet factory to guided instruction and collaborative learning is simple or smooth; however, we believe it is far more difficult for educators and far more costly to students to maintain the status quo.

What It Is & What It Isn't

Promoting Successful Practice

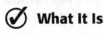 What It Is

Guiding students as they learn and practice new concepts and skills

> Example: A kindergarten teacher works to guide children to retell the major events of a story in proper sequence. The teacher reads the story once and then leads the students in discussing the important events in the story. Students have difficulty ascertaining which events were important. The teacher explains that one way to decide if an event was important is to determine if the ending might have been different if the event did not occur. As students mention various events, the teacher helps them use this decision rule in deciding if the event was important. The teacher reads the story a second time and asks students to raise their hands when they hear the teacher mention one of the important events they had discussed. As students identify the important events, the teacher hands children large hand-drawn picture cards that represent each event. The teacher asks students to explain which major events came before and after each event discussed. The teacher models and directs students to practice describing the various events in complete sentences. When the story is finished, the teacher asks all of the students with picture cards to stand up and organize themselves in proper sequence. The students who do not have picture cards are asked to check to be sure the pictures are in the proper sequence. Individual students are then asked to share their major events in proper sequence.

⊗ What It Isn't

Quickly pushing students to work independently

> Example: A kindergarten teacher works to guide children to retell the major events of a story in proper sequence. The teacher reads the story to the students and notes the important events. The teacher discusses the order in which the events occurred, using words like *first*, *second*, *third*, and *last*. Then the teacher sends students back to their seats to color pictures that represent the major events in the story (without evidence that they are ready to work independently). Students must then cut out the pictures and paste them on construction paper in the proper sequence.

⊘ What It Is

Guiding students in ways that help them through the struggling necessary to understand challenging concepts

A fifth-grade teacher works to build her students' understanding of multiplying a whole number by a decimal. The teacher writes a problem on the board (512 × 0.25) and asks students what the problem means. Students read the problem accurately; however, the teacher asks students to explain more precisely what the problem means. As students struggle, the teacher asks, "What is 25 hundredths?" When students do not respond, she asks, "Is 25 hundredths larger or smaller than one?" Several students answer, "Smaller," prompting the teacher to ask, "How much smaller? Talk to your shoulder partner and decide." After students have discussed the issue, the teacher asks one student, who explains that 25 hundredths is a lot smaller than 1 because 25 hundredths is really like 25 cents out of a dollar. "Good!" the teacher exclaims. "So, if you multiply 512 by a number smaller than 1, will the product be larger than 512 or smaller than 512?" Students decide that the product should be a lot smaller than 512. Then the teacher explains that because one of the factors is smaller than 1, one way they can check to make sure that their answer is reasonable is to check to see if the product is considerably smaller than 512. Then, the teacher asks students to explain how they would multiply 512 and 25. Several students explain the algorithm, one step at a time. Frequently, the teacher asks, "Why?" when a student explains a step. The students explain correctly because of their prior instruction. When students have finished the problem and arrive at a product, the teacher asks a student, "Is this a reasonable answer to the problem 512 × 0.25?" The student answers, "No." The teacher asks another student, "Why?" The student explains that the product is far more than 512. Then the teacher asks if they did something wrong in calculating. One student explains that they did not do anything wrong. They simply multiplied 512 × 25. They did not multiply 512 × 0.25. The teacher reminds the students of the importance of place value as they multiply two whole numbers. She then explains how they can account for the place value of decimals in factors when they generate a product. Using the simple procedure of counting digits to the right of the decimal, the teacher helps students find the place for the decimal in the product. Then she asks, "Why does that procedure make sense? Talk with your partner." Some students note that the product is now smaller than 512, suggesting that they actually multiplied by a number smaller than 1. Others suggest that if you multiply by a hundredth, the number generated through the algorithm has to be divisible by 100.

Ⓧ What It Isn't

Presenting the easy concepts and allowing students to struggle independently with the more difficult concepts

Example: A fifth-grade teacher works to build her students' under-standing of multiplying a whole number by a decimal. The teacher writes a problem on the board (512 × 0.25) and asks students to copy it. Then the teacher demonstrates how to solve the problem using a common multiplication algorithm. As the teacher moves through the problem, she occasionally asks, "What's the next step?" The same two students answer each time, while others remain silent. After the multiplication is finished, the teacher points to the second factor and asks, "How many digits are to the right of the decimal point up here?" The same students correctly respond, "Two." Then the teacher explains that there must be two digits to the right of the decimal in the product. The teacher explains, "See, this is easy. You already know how to do this because you know how to multiply. You just have to remember to count the number of digits to the right of the decimal in the factors and make sure you have the same number of digits to the right of the decimal in the product." Then the teacher assigns items one through twenty in the textbook. Students work on those independently; however, some students struggle. None of the students correctly answers items nineteen and twenty: the two "Think Big Questions." These questions ask students to explain in a short narrative response why their answers to the first two problems (items one and two) are logical and reasonable.

✓ What It Is

Monitoring student performance as students complete independent work

Example: After teaching his seventh-grade students how some authors use precise verbs to influence the mood of a story, the teacher asks students to annotate a passage and note the mood created/influenced by the author's choice of verbs. After giving the assign-ment, the teacher circulates and observes students working. The teacher notes that most students are performing well; however, three students are missing important examples of verbs that influ-ence mood. Also, the three students are making annotations about words that are not verbs. The teacher quietly asks these three students to join him at his desk. While the other students continue to work independently, the teacher guides the three students through the assignment.

✗ What It Isn't

Assigning independent work without monitoring student performance

Example: After teaching his seventh-grade students how some authors use precise verbs to influence the mood of a story, the teacher asks students to annotate a passage and note the mood created/influenced by the author's choice of verbs. After giving the assignment, the teacher returns to his desk and begins correcting last night's homework papers.

✅ What It Is

Building students' capacity to monitor their own progress in completing assignments well

> Example: A seventh-grade social studies teacher requires students to write a paper that compares and contrasts life in the Middle Ages with life during the Renaissance. The teacher guides the students in creating Venn diagrams that illustrate the ways in which life was similar and different during these two time periods. Before students begin the writing assignment, the teacher passes out four unmarked, nonidentifiable sample papers for this assignment from students in prior years. In small groups, the students critique the papers and discuss what makes them interesting and informative. Through the students' critique, the teacher guides the students in creating a rubric for their assignment. Once the rubric is created, the teacher explains how she will use the rubric to grade student papers. Then the teacher asks students to discuss how they can use the rubric to help them create outstanding papers.

❌ What It Isn't

Assuming that students have the capacity to monitor their own progress in completing assignments well

> Example: A seventh-grade social studies teacher requires students to write a paper that compares and contrasts life in the Middle Ages with life during the Renaissance. After spending a class period discussing each era, students begin working independently to complete the assignment while the teacher works to respond to e-mail requests from the district office. She directs the students to approach her desk if they have questions.

✅ What It Is

Providing students independent work they are likely to perceive as interesting and/or worth completing

> Example: After a lesson on converting fractions to percentages and decimals, a teacher gives every student a copy of a newspaper clipping, including the current batting statistics (number of at bats, number of hits, and batting averages) for all members of the local baseball team. For homework, students are required to select one player and determine what the player's batting average would be if the player successfully hit during the next five, ten, twenty, and fifty at bats. The teacher engages students in a discussion of how they could go about making such a calculation. Students are

encouraged to write down the necessary steps in the process. Then the teacher asks various students to read a step and explain the rationale for each one. When the teacher is convinced that students know how to proceed, they are dismissed.

(X) What It Isn't

Providing students "busywork" or assignments they are likely to perceive as either repetitive and dull or far too difficult to complete successfully

Example: After a lesson on converting fractions to percentages and decimals, a teacher assigns, as homework, page 128 from the math book. The page includes thirty problems that require students to convert fractions into percentages or decimals and one "Think Big Question" that requires students to read and answer a word problem requiring the conversion of fractions to percentages and decimals. Immediately, several more capable students groan, whispering to their neighbors about how boring it will be to complete thirty-one uninteresting problems. In contrast, a less capable student sighs and frowns, writing on the bottom of her paper, so her neighbor can see, "I don't even know how to start the first one."

Practice Guide Related to Promoting Successful Practice

For information on possible uses of this practice guide, please see pages 5–6 in Chapter 1.

Table 7.1

1. Did the teacher check at least 25 percent of the students to ensure they understood the concept before allowing independent practice?	Ⓨ	Ⓝ
2. At least 50 percent?	Ⓨ	Ⓝ
3. At least 75 percent?	Ⓨ	Ⓝ
4. Prior to giving students independent work, did the teacher check to ensure that students had developed a depth of understanding of key concepts?	Ⓨ	Ⓝ
5. Prior to giving students independent work, did the teacher check to ensure that students understood the directions?	Ⓨ	Ⓝ
6. Did students learn strategies for checking their work and assessing their mastery?	Ⓨ	Ⓝ
7. Did the teacher monitor independent practice to ensure student mastery?	Ⓨ	Ⓝ
8. Did the teacher provide individual assistance when needed?	Ⓨ	Ⓝ
9. Did the teacher work with small groups of students when needed?	Ⓨ	Ⓝ
10. If several students made serious errors in independent practice, did the teacher stop and reteach?	Ⓨ	Ⓝ

11. If students worked independently, did at least 80 percent get at least 80 percent of the task correct?   Ⓨ   Ⓝ

12. Prior to giving homework, did the teacher ensure that students were likely to be able to complete the assignment successfully?   Ⓨ   Ⓝ

In a strong lesson, a "yes" answer is recorded for at least six of these items.
In an outstanding lesson, a "yes" answer is recorded for at least nine of these items.

Practical Next Steps

1. In collaboration with teacher colleagues, engage in a book study of *Better Learning through Structured Teaching: A Framework for the Gradual Release of Responsibility* (2nd edition) (Fisher & Frey, 2014).

2. In collaboration with colleagues, plan your teaching of the next important student learning goal to include specific strategies for providing focused instruction, guided instruction, collaborative learning, and independent learning. In particular, decide how you and your colleagues will determine that your students are ready to move successfully from one level to the next. Also, consider how you might prepare to differentiate instruction when you determine that students are at different levels of understanding.

3. Before handing out the next class assignment, make predictions of how each student will perform. Instead of giving the assignment to all students, only give the assignment to those you predict will perform well. Engage the other students in guided instruction or cooperative learning to increase the likelihood that students will learn the concept or skill well before they pursue independent practice.

4. When you provide students the next independent learning task, take five to ten minutes to monitor how students are performing independently. If you find that some students are answering many problems incorrectly, pull those students aside into a guided instruction group. If you find that all students are answering many problems incorrectly, stop the independent practice and provide more focused instruction. Use the students' errors as teaching tools.

5. Before giving the next homework assignment, review the assignment carefully. Determine how few of the problems you would need students to answer in order to assess each student's level of mastery. Reduce the assignment accordingly.

References

Fisher, D., & Frey, N. (2014). *Better learning through structured teaching: A framework for the gradual release of responsibility* (2nd ed.). Alexandria, VA: Association for Supervision and Curriculum Development.

Hattie, J. A. C. (2009). *Visible learning: A synthesis of over 800 meta-analyses relating to achievement*. Abingdon, Oxon: Routledge.

Hill, J. D., & Flynn, K. M. (2006). *Classroom instruction that works with English language learners*. Alexandria, VA: Association for Supervision and Curriculum Development.

Marzano, R. J. (2010). *The art and science of teaching: A comprehensive framework for effective instruction*. Alexandria, VA: Association for Supervision and Curriculum Development.

Pearson, P. D., & Gallagher, M. C. (1983). The instruction of reading comprehension. *Contemporary Educational Psychology, 8,* 317–344.

Rosenshine, B. (1983). Teaching functions in instructional programs. *The Elementary School Journal, 83*(4), 335–351.

Tomlinson, C. A., & Moon, T. R. (2013). *Assessment and student success in a differentiated classroom*. Alexandria, VA: Association for Supervision and Curriculum Development.

8 Leading Students to Love Learning

The fourth-grade students waited patiently in their white lab jackets as a teacher gave each small group a real pig heart. The three teachers had brought their students into one classroom as they worked together to teach this lesson that combined objectives related to the circulatory system, metric measurement, and data analysis. Like all lessons at Southside Elementary in Miami, Florida, this one centered upon a physical object (in this case, a pig's heart) that students could touch and manipulate.

"What do you remember about how the heart is divided?" one teacher asked, calling upon students to talk with each other and recall their learning from the previous lesson.

"The heart is divided into parts," one student told his teammates.

"Yeah, they're called chambers," another student explained.

"Today, you're going inside the heart to see the chambers," the teacher stated enthusiastically. "But first, we need your team to collect as much data as possible about your pig heart. As scientists, you want to collect specific information that will help you know more about this particular pig heart. What are some kinds of data that you might collect about your pig heart? Talk with your teammates and list some kinds of data."

The students generated a list of ideas, including color, weight, width, length, and circumference, reflecting their prior knowledge from both mathematics and other science lab activities. The teachers then gave each group a lab sheet that required them to collect various observations about their pig heart. The teachers engaged the students in discussions of the metric measurements that would work best to record precise information about their pig hearts. The teachers also got students to discuss how they could make sure their measurements were accurate.

"We have to make sure that the weight scale is at zero when it's empty," one student offered.

"When we make linear measurements, we have to start at zero, and if we're counting the big lines [on the measuring tape], we have to make sure we're counting by the right number," another student explained.

The groups collected, checked, and double checked their measurements and recorded them on their lab sheets. Then the groups began comparing to determine which heart was biggest, heaviest, longest, and so on. Students generated questions that teachers challenged students to answer.

"So why isn't the heart very red?" one student asked.

"Good question," a teacher responded. "What do you think? Talk about it with your groups."

"Maybe pig hearts aren't the same color as human hearts," one student suggested.

"I think it's because there's other stuff covering the heart," another student suggested.

One student went to the website her class had explored previously and found that fat and tissue surrounded the heart. She shared the information with the class.

"What do you think you'll see when we bisect the heart?" one of the teachers asked. Some of the students guessed that they would see blood. Others predicted they would see valves. Others expected to see chambers. Next, a teacher went to each group and used a sharp knife to cut the heart into two halves.

The students watched in awe.

"Wow, I see the chambers!" a boy exclaimed.

"It looks just like the website!" another noted.

"Does my heart look like this?" another asked.

The teachers directed students back to their lab sheets and asked them to collect more data about the chambers.

Southside Elementary Museums Magnet School is in the Miami-Dade County School District in Miami, Florida. The school serves approximately 800 students in grades pre-kindergarten through five. The school won the America's Best Urban Schools Award in 2008.

A Perpetual Question

On the Minds of Educators Striving to Produce Equity and Excellence

How can I get each and every one of my students to think, "I love learning about this! I can't wait to learn even more"?

In high-performing urban schools, students are more likely to understand and master challenging academic content, in part because students learn to love learning. Teachers create learning environments that are interesting and exciting. Students willingly (and even eagerly) dedicate their time, thinking, and energy to learning, solving problems, accomplishing goals, and attaining deep understanding of concepts and skills. While not every lesson is as powerful as the heart bisection described at the beginning of this chapter, a variety of lesson characteristics magnify student interest in learning. Certainly, in our observations of high-performing urban schools, we saw few lessons that might be considered dull, monotonous, or overly repetitive. Consistently, students were eager to attend classes. Students were excited about what they were learning.

By leading students to love learning, educators completed the circle illustrated in Figure 8.1 in a manner that maximized the impact of the other outer-ring practices, heightened the focus on understanding and mastery, and powerfully affirmed to students that they were both valued and capable.

To lead students to love learning, teachers in high-performing schools exhibited sincere enthusiasm for the content they were teaching and for the students they were serving. Teachers deliberately helped their students understand how the content they were learning was relevant to their current and future lives. As well, teachers employed project-based, problem-based, inquiry-based, and experiential learning opportunities. Additionally, teachers integrated the arts, technology, and physical education into their teaching of core academic content and maximized opportunities for student-to-student interaction in learning processes. Finally, teachers provided opportunities for students to excel with challenging academic content.

Figure 8.1

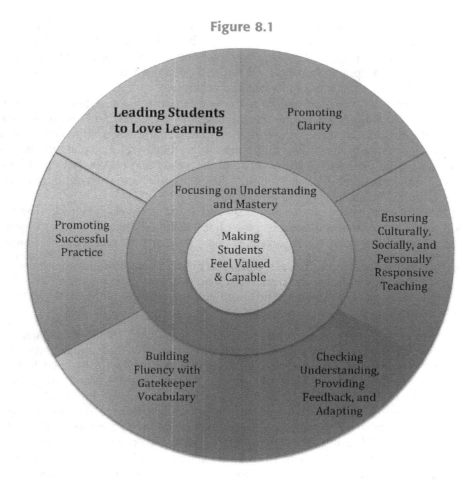

Teaching Enthusiastically

Students are more likely to learn when teachers evidence enthusiasm for the content they teach. Hattie (2009) suggested that while teacher passion is rarely studied empirically, "it infuses many of the influences that make the difference . . ." (p. 24). Enthusiastic, passionate teaching increases the impact of teaching practices, including each of the practices described in this book. For example, when teachers at William Bryant School in Cleveland, Ohio; Uplift Education Peak Prep in Dallas, Texas; or Feaster Charter School in Chula Vista, California, were checking understanding, providing feedback, and adapting, they passionately sought to understand what their students knew. When teachers at Harriet Tubman Blue Ribbon School in Newark, New Jersey; William Dandy Middle School in Fort Lauderdale, Florida; or Revere High School in Boston, Massachusetts, enthusiastically taught lessons that were culturally, socially, and personally relevant to their students, the evidence of student understanding and mastery seemed to skyrocket. When teachers at Patrick Henry Preparatory School in New York City enthusiastically promoted clarity about learning outcomes and success criteria through their lesson plan template, exemplars, and expectations checklist and grading rubrics, the impact on student success was stunning. In high-performing urban schools, we observed many examples of the eight teaching practices described in this book, and we also observed many examples of the practices being implemented ardently.

Through their enthusiasm, teachers transmitted their love of subject areas to their students. At Fallon Park Elementary in Roanoke, Virginia, students spoke passionately about their work building volcanoes, conducting electricity experiments, and completing atom projects. Two girls sang a song they had learned about circumference and radius. Students proudly spoke of the hands-on projects they completed at school. "Teachers let us do experiments," they explained and then added, "Teachers make it fun. My teacher talks in an exciting voice."

In many classrooms at Dayton Business and Technology High School, students learned to love academic content areas they had previously hated. Teacher passion and enthusiasm were compelling forces for many students. As one student shared:

> At this school, every day, in each class, teachers do something to make the subject real. They show you how what you're learning is practical. They show you how you can use it. They help you see why they love it. So, you start to love it, too.

In high-performing urban schools, teachers exhibited their enthusiasm for their students even more than they exhibited enthusiasm for their subject areas. We observed the sincere, proud smiles of kindergarten teachers who listened to their students read sentences independently with understanding. We watched a middle school math teacher give avid high-fives after listening to students explain their multistep solutions to real-world problems. We saw the gleam in the eye of a government teacher as she looked over a student's shoulder who accurately scored his essay as a perfect "5" using a rigorous rubric. We saw fist pumping and heard celebratory shouting from a team of sixth-grade science teachers as they recognized that each of their students mastered the formative assessment given the week prior. Teachers were enthusiastic because they cared deeply about their students. Specifically, they cared deeply about their students succeeding in school and life. Their enthusiasm was obvious to outside observers. Most likely, their enthusiasm was even more obvious to their students.

Teaching enthusiastically requires energy, but it also transfers energy. In many classrooms in high-performing urban schools, the energy was palpable. One teacher at Signal Hill Elementary in Long Beach, California, explained, "I make sure my students are exhausted by the end of the day. They work hard all day long. We're constantly moving. And, of course, this means that [by the end of the day] I'm exhausted, too."

Highlighting Relevance

In high-performing urban schools, teachers help students understand the importance of the content being taught. As students at Franklin Town Charter High in Philadelphia, Pennsylvania, explained, "Here, we learn things that we will need in college and in life." Students are more likely to love learning when they understand the relevance of the content.

Frequently, when we observed classrooms in high-performing urban schools, we interrupted students and asked them what they were learning. When they answered, we followed up by asking why they were learning the content they described. First, it is important to note that typically students explained the lesson objective accurately and often with great detail. Second, it was common for students to share rationale such as, "We're going to need to be able to understand this in order to understand computers or become engineers" or "I need to know this in order to succeed in college" or "This is important because this was a real event and it could happen again in my lifetime."

Teachers took time to explain why their learning objective was important to their students. Teachers helped students understand how the lesson could influence their lives currently or in the near future. For example, an algebra teacher at Hambrick Middle School in Houston, Texas, explained:

> If your employer paid you by the hour and gave you a bonus for good work, you might need to use a linear equation to help you make sure that your paycheck was accurate. Who wants to learn how to use a linear equation to make sure your paycheck includes all the money you are owed?

Instantly, Hambrick students decided this objective was critically important. Students decided that they *needed* to understand. (And not just for the purpose of performing well on the state assessment.) Although teachers deliberately ensured that students learned the most important content included on state examinations, they offered students more powerful reasons for engaging and wanting to learn.

Often teachers enhanced student perceptions of relevance by making concepts seem real to students. For example, at Mueller Charter School in Chula Vista, California, seventh-grade students spent one day each week at a nature center, where they engaged in real science activities with real scientists. The activities helped students learn about issues that influence local ecosystems in important ways. Kensler and Uline (2017) demonstrated the potential for green schools, schools that practice whole-school sustainability, to maximize student learning, while at the same time cultivating stronger, healthier local communities and reducing the school's ecological footprint.

In various classrooms throughout the country, we observed students acting out activities related to the three branches of government, using food to solve problems with fractions, writing letters to real people in response to real issues, charting and graphing student preferences and accomplishments, and using a wide array of manipulatives. Teachers helped students understand complex abstract concepts by using concrete objects and examples that were highly relevant to students' lives.

Using Project-Based, Problem-Based, and Experiential Learning

In many high-performing urban schools, students learned to love learning because learning was structured in ways that required students to complete projects, solve problems, and experience real-world phenomena.

Boss and Larmer (2018, p. 1) defined project-based learning in a way that incorporated many concepts associated with problem-based, inquiry-based, or experiential learning. Specifically, they described project-based learning as:

> a proven framework to help students be better equipped to tackle future challenges.
>
> Through academically rigorous projects, students acquire deep content knowledge while also mastering 21st century success skills: knowing how to think critically, analyze information for reliability, collaborate with diverse colleagues, and solve problems creatively.

In many high-performing urban schools, teachers used project-based learning extensively. While maintaining a focus on what they wanted students to understand and master, teachers (1) built a culture that supported students' independence, fostered collaboration, supported risk taking, and encouraged high-quality work; (2) designed and planned a blueprint for the project, including formative and summative assessments; (3) ensured that the project was aligned to important standards and learning goals; (4) managed activities to facilitate students achieving deep learning; (5) assessed student learning to ensure that all students advanced toward mastery; (6) scaffolded student learning so every student was likely to succeed; and (7) engaged with and coached students in a manner that nurtured a caring, trusting relationship (Boss & Larmer, 2018). Barron and Darling-Hammond (2008) emphasized that through project-based learning and similar approaches, learning environments can advance student understanding in reading, mathematics, science, and other subjects.

In many high-performing urban schools, project-based learning dominated approaches to teaching science and mathematics. At Young Men's Leadership Academy in Fort Worth, Texas, students engaged in Project Lead the Way and other interdisciplinary projects that featured hands-on learning opportunities. Similarly at Engineering and Science University Magnet School in New Haven, Connecticut (another Project Lead the Way school), students benefitted from thematic, interdisciplinary, project-based learning. At Rose Park Math and Science Magnet Middle School in Nashville, Tennessee, science, technology, engineering, and mathematics were embedded throughout the curricula with interdisciplinary, project-based lessons that emphasized problem solving and critical thinking. At Mittie Pullam Elementary in Brownsville, Texas, students received science instruction through technology, interactive lessons, investigations, and hands-on activities. At Pershing Elementary in Dallas, Texas, students grew and harvested crops, observed the butterfly cycle, harvested rainwater, composted and fertilized planting beds, observed, and studied a fish pond, and learned about xeriscaping. Students at Hillside University Demonstration School in San Bernardino, California, engaged in project-based learning to deepen their understanding of a wide array of concepts related to social studies, science, and language arts.

In other high-performing urban schools, project-based learning approaches were observed throughout all curricular areas. For example, at the World of Inquiry School in Rochester, New York, students constantly engaged in projects that helped them learn important concepts related to English and social studies, as well as mathematics, science, and other academic subjects. At Spring Creek Elementary in Garland, Texas, project-based, experiential lessons were designed to augment lessons and create real-world opportunities for students to apply what they learned. At Southside Museums School in Miami, every lesson was enhanced through a project or an object that students had the opportunity to explore and manipulate. At Mary Walke Stephens Elementary in Houston, student progress was monitored through project-based assessments designed to ensure that students could apply key academic concepts in English/language arts, mathematics, and other subject areas. In these schools, projects were not merely activities to promote student interest. They were vehicles designed to enhance student understanding and mastery.

Integrating the Arts, Technology, and Physical Education Throughout Curricula

In high-performing urban schools, teachers enriched academic lessons through the integration of the arts, technology, and physical education. While teachers focused deliberately on important academic objectives in science, mathematics, English, and social studies, they made learning more interesting and powerful through the integration of the arts, technology, and physical education.

In recent years, we have found struggling urban schools where educators and policy makers decided to sacrifice the arts and physical education so students would have double doses of mathematics, English, and reading. In contrast, almost all of the high-performing urban schools we studied had well-developed programs in art, music, drama, dance, and physical education. In particular, the Chula Vista Elementary School District in the San Diego area (home to several America's Best Urban Schools Award winners) committed $15 million to increase visual and performing arts instruction for the district's students.

In many other high-performing urban schools, we found rich programs in the arts. For example, at Osceola Creek Middle School in Palm Beach County, Florida, more than one-fourth of the school's 690 students participated in the instrumental music program. At A.B. Anderson Academy in Houston, Texas, all students participated in a fine arts program that included dance, violin, art, choir, and drama. At Cerritos Elementary in Glendale, California, students received instrumental music lessons four days each week from professional musicians. At Daniel Breeden Elementary, ballroom dancing was just one of the offerings that excited students about the arts. At Hillside University Demonstration School in San Bernardino, students benefitted from a comprehensive music program that included instruction in music theory. In addition to overall strong programs, in the high-performing urban schools, student learning was enhanced by the integration of the arts, technology, and physical education into core academic instruction.

At schools such as Harriet Tubman in Newark, New Jersey, and Dreamkeepers Academy in Norfolk, Virginia, the use of drama and music helped students learn important concepts related to history, English, mathematics, and science. Music and dance were important tools for teaching academic concepts at Muller Elementary in Tampa, Florida, and at Escontrias Elementary in El Paso, Texas. Teachers at Charles Lunsford Elementary in Rochester, New York, used physical education activities to reinforce concepts related to Venn diagrams. At R.N. Harris Integrated Arts School in Durham, North Carolina, students regularly demonstrated mastery of academic content through theatrical displays, tableaux (in which participants make still images with their bodies to represent a scene), dance, visual arts, and music.

At William Cullen Bryant in Cleveland, Ohio, the eighth-grade math teacher engaged students in discussions of artwork by Ellsworth Kelly, reflecting on various mathematical concepts represented in the artwork, such as symmetry, dimension, and scale. Then she asked students to create pieces in a similar style, using up to six different colors. Next, the teacher engaged the students in calculating the ratios of their use of different colors and expressing those ratios with fractions, decimals, and percentages.

At Uplift Education Peak Preparatory High School in Dallas, Texas, the eleventh-grade writing teacher used the work of a graffiti artist to help students understand how rhetorical devices can be used to achieve a specific purpose with an audience. Students learned that just as the graffiti artist used specific devices to lead viewers to think, feel, and react, they could use specific rhetorical devices to help their readers think, feel, and react.

Educators recognized that students were more likely to understand and appreciate challenging academic concepts when they saw those concepts reflected in other disciplines. Thus, we saw several examples of teachers using art to reinforce student understanding of geometric concepts. We saw students gaining a deeper understanding of fractions as they learned to read measures of music. We saw students acting out scenes in which historical events were reenacted.

Students enthusiastically engaged in mathematics, science, social studies, and English lessons when art, music, or drama provided avenues for connecting the academic content with their cultural, social, and personal backgrounds. Students understood and remembered the historical events they acted out in short plays. Students begged their teachers to allow them to continue working when they were converting classic Greek tragedies into hip-hop poems they would perform. As third-grade students played kickball, they quickly calculated and remembered multiplication facts when the teacher made each score worth six points.

Similarly, we observed teachers integrating the use of technology in the teaching of important academic concepts. Students used smart boards and clickers abundantly throughout the school day at Ira Harbison Elementary in National City, California. Students at Escontrias Elementary in El Paso used iPods to help them practice reading skills. In many schools, we saw students using the Internet to access information, acquire diverse perspectives, resolve disputes about facts, and visit distant places. It is important to note that teachers structured lessons so that students were manipulating the technology (not simply watching the teacher use the technology). As well, it is important to note that teachers did not pursue the use of technology simply to provide students an experience with technology. Instead, teachers used technology to help students better understand the academic objectives they wanted students to learn. Most often, technology was not simply a worksheet on a computer monitor. Instead, applications engaged students in designing, creating, researching, and exploring.

At Eastlake High School in El Paso, many teachers adopted a blended-learning approach to instruction that combined online educational materials and opportunities with traditional place-based classroom methods. Other Eastlake teachers adopted a flipped instructional model where the course content was delivered to students through a combination of videos, podcasts, click-through lessons, and other technologies outside the instructional day. As a result, more class time was reserved for activities that engaged students in collaborative, authentic, hands-on activities.

Revere High School in Boston, Massachusetts, also developed a student-centered flipped learning model. Technology was ubiquitous at Revere High as teachers and students used iPads and other devices to acquire and present information, collaborate, and chart progress. At Revere, students who were certified technology experts sat at a "Genius Bar" in the learning commons to offer troubleshooting services to both faculty and students throughout the school day.

Similarly, at Maplewood Richmond Heights High School in St. Louis, every student was given a device. Students used their devices regularly to research, collaborate, and develop presentations of their learning. Like Revere, Maplewood Richmond Heights had a student-run "Genius Bar."

At Keller Dual Immersion Middle School in Long Beach, California, each student had an iPad that was used continuously to complete projects. For example, in lessons devoted to teaching persuasive essay writing, students created persuasive commercials that incorporated their writing. As students in one class learned to write biographies, they used iMovie to create documentaries.

In many schools, such as Wynnebrook Elementary in West Palm Beach, Florida, teachers used technology to tailor learning experiences to students' interests and needs. McCullen (2003) emphasized how teachers could use technology to differentiate instruction and present content in ways that aligned with students' needs. The use of technology often helped teachers ensure that all of their diverse learners made strong academic progress. Hug, Krajcik, and Marx (2005) explained how interactive learning technologies, embedded within extended project-based science curriculum units, increased the engagement of urban middle school students in actively learning key science concepts. They urged educators to incorporate learning technologies within science instruction to advance equity and promote learning among diverse learners.

Maximizing Student-to-Student Engagement

Barron and Darling-Hammond (2008) described how "collaborative approaches to learning are beneficial for individual and collective knowledge growth" (p. 35). In the award-winning schools we studied, we found that students were learning to love learning as they engaged with each other.

Students enjoy interacting with their peers. In high-performing urban schools, teachers skillfully provided students structured opportunities to talk with and engage their peers around specific academic objectives. For example, at Montgomery Elementary in Chula Vista, California, teachers frequently structured cooperative learning activities or other activities in which students discussed important academic concepts with their peers. At B.L. Gray Junior High School in Sharyland, Texas, teachers intentionally planned lessons to ensure that students engaged in academic discourse with each other. At O'Farrell Charter School in San Diego, students would become so absorbed in their academic conversations with peers that they would complain when the class periods ended.

In elementary, middle, and high schools, we saw many examples of teachers structuring conversations that required students to discuss, explain, teach, and debate. At all grade levels, we observed examples of cooperative learning in which students worked in teams to help each other reach deeper understandings of lesson objectives. Typically, in high-performing urban schools, we heard student voices more than we heard teacher voices. However, classroom environments were not chaotic. Students engaged each other to fulfill a specific purpose. Teachers gave students a reason to collaborate, share their thinking, and learn from each other.

Student-to-student collaboration often created opportunities for students to assume formal and informal leadership roles in the learning process. Even as early as kindergarten, children at C.E. Rose Elementary in Tucson, Arizona, learned to assume leadership roles in lessons. At schools such as Samuel Dupont Elementary in Brooklyn, reciprocal teaching strategies provided every student opportunities to assume leadership roles with their peers. Teachers were creative in establishing circumstances that gave many students opportunities to share their academic strengths. As a result, students learned to perceive themselves as academically capable. They learned to love learning.

Providing Students Opportunities to Excel With Challenging Content

Many students who attended high-performing urban schools had excellent opportunities to excel with challenging academic content. Often, students had opportunities to learn concepts and skills that few urban students learn. Students expressed pride in their academic accomplishments. They saw themselves as capable of learning, understanding, and exceling with advanced academic content.

In high-performing urban elementary schools, children were proud that they were learning impressive academic skills. Students at John Quincy Adams Elementary in Dallas, Texas, were justifiably proud of their understanding of algebraic concepts. Students at Highland Elementary School in Silver Spring, Maryland, and Branch Brook School in Newark, New Jersey, knew that their essay writing skills were far beyond grade level. Students at Westcliff Elementary School in Fort Worth, Texas, exuded confidence in their ability to explain the scientific relationships they examined in their science experiments. Students at Finney Elementary in Chula Vista, California, were proud of the novels they were reading and understanding. They were thrilled about their successes using sentence frames, phrase starters, and text structures to create compositions that resembled the work of middle school students. At Sylvan Rodriguez Elementary in Houston, students eagerly researched global issues in preparation for their International Baccalaureate exhibition. At George Washington Elementary in Chicago, Illinois, students were excited to have opportunities to learn Mandarin Chinese. Throughout high-performing urban schools, even young students recognized that they were learning concepts and skills that many elementary school children do not have the opportunity to acquire.

At Patrick Henry Preparatory School, P.S./I.S. 171 in New York City, one sixth-grade student explained, "I've only been at this school a few weeks and I think I've already learned more than I learned at my old school because the curriculum is very challenging." This sentiment was expressed by dozens of students in almost every high-performing urban school we visited. Students recognized that they were learning content that would propel them to new opportunities they could barely imagine.

In high-performing urban middle schools, students knew that they were learning content that was preparing them to excel in high school. At both McLean Middle School and Stripling Middle School in Fort Worth, Texas, over half of the students were enrolled in Pre-Advanced Placement and honors classes. Additionally, students had the opportunity to earn high school credits in disciplines such as biology, geometry, and English. Many McLean students proceeded to high school and became National Merit Semifinalists and National Hispanic Scholars, providing additional evidence of the power of their middle school preparation. Similarly, at Stripling Middle School in Fort Worth, the rigorous middle school offerings accelerated students' progress toward college.

At Hialeah Gardens Middle School in Miami, Florida, students chose from six academies: biomedical, agrosciences, engineering, law, arts and entertainment, and information technology. The academies presented challenging academic content in ways that helped students perceive themselves as capable middle school students who would proceed to become capable high school students and, ultimately, capable college graduates.

In high-performing urban high schools, students received many opportunities to learn challenging academic content. Many of the high schools offered dual-credit or early-college programs. These programs allowed students to earn high school and college credits simultaneously through courses offered either at the high school or on nearby college campuses. For example, at Mission Early College High School in El Paso, almost all of the graduating seniors expected that they would have already earned associate degrees when they completed high school. Trinidad Garza Early College High School in Dallas; the Middle College at UNCG, in Greensboro, North Carolina; and Veterans Memorial Early College High School and Pace Early College High School in Brownsville, Texas, are also examples of schools that have successfully utilized dual-credit programs to challenge their students.

Other high-performing urban high schools provided their students substantial Advanced Placement offerings. For example, Eastlake High School in El Paso, Texas, offered students sixteen different Advanced Placement courses, along with eight dual-enrollment opportunities. At Thurgood Marshall Academy Public Charter High School in Washington, DC, students took many Advanced Placement courses and scored well on Advanced Placement exams.

In many high-performing urban high schools, high levels of academic expectation were also evident in general curriculum courses. For example, at Maplewood Richmond Heights High School in St. Louis and Doral Academy Preparatory School in Miami, Florida, students knew they were being prepared for college and careers even when they took courses that were not identified as Advanced Placement or honors courses.

It is important to note that at many of the high-performing urban secondary schools, teachers offered very challenging courses, but they also offered supports designed to help students succeed in the challenging courses. In some of the high-performing schools, teachers designed and implemented their own programs to help increase the likelihood that students would succeed in rigorous courses. Teachers planned and implemented programs to teach students excellent study skills and note-taking skills. Teachers designed curricula to help students read and understand challenging texts. They sought to increase the likelihood that every student who took an honors, Advanced Placement, or dual-credit course would successfully learn the content and look forward to learning more.

In many other high-performing urban schools, including Rafael Hernando III Middle School, Eastlake High School, and America High School in El Paso, Texas; Marine Creek Collegiate High School in Fort Worth, Texas; and O'Farrell Charter School in San Diego, California, educators adopted the AVID program (Advancement Via Individual Determination) to support their students as they pursued challenging academic courses. AVID emphasizes teaching practices, classroom activities, and academic behaviors that help students recognize their capacity to succeed academically while simultaneously building students' capacity to succeed in challenging academic environments.

Students were motivated to succeed when they had opportunities to learn content that was unquestionably rigorous. However, educators recognized that they needed to sustain student motivation by ensuring students had the quantity and quality of support they needed to succeed with rigorous academic content.

Summary

In high-performing urban schools, students learned more, in part because they learned to love learning. Students' love for learning was influenced first by enthusiastic teaching. Students were excited about learning when they realized that their teachers were passionate about the academic content and when they realized that their teachers were committed to their success. Also, students were more likely to love learning when their teachers found ways to accentuate how the academic content was relevant to the students.

Additionally, we found that teachers increased students' love for learning by planning project-based lessons that helped students learn key academic standards through interesting, hands-on approaches. As well, teachers integrated the arts, technology, and physical education into the teaching of core academic content in ways that heightened student interest and engagement.

Teachers recognized that students of all ages love to interact with their peers. So throughout high-performing urban schools, teachers made abundant use of cooperative learning approaches that helped students learn challenging academic content while they worked with their peers.

Finally, in high-performing urban schools, educators recognized that human beings love feeling successful. Instead of limiting students to low-level or mediocre curricula, educators provided opportunities for students to see themselves as capable of learning challenging academic content. Teachers provided their students rigorous academic content, and they provided their students the quantity and quality of support needed so students could successfully understand and master the rigorous academic content.

What It Is & What It Isn't

Leading Students to Love Learning

 **What It Is**

Teaching enthusiastically

Example: The teacher began a review of metric measurement concepts the fourth graders had learned. "Remind me of times you might need to know something about metric linear measurements." Students quickly gave answers that included references to foreign travel, the use of tools, watching the Olympics or other sporting events, repairing a car engine, and so on. The teacher responded, "Yes, those are great examples! And you're going to be ready to do all those things and more, because you know a lot about metric linear measurements." To demonstrate to the students they had learned a significant amount, the teacher began asking questions such as, "Which is longer: a centimeter or an inch? Is an inch a little longer or a lot longer than a centimeter? How many centimeters are in an inch? Which tool would be longer: a one-inch wrench or a one-centimeter wrench? Which is longer: a yard or a meter? Which race would be longer: a hundred-yard dash or a hundred-meter dash? How much longer? How could you figure it out?" The teacher asked the questions quickly and responded positively whenever students answer correctly. "You are becoming experts in metric linear measurement!" the teacher exclaimed. "I'm proud of you. I think you're ready to learn about metric liquid measurements!"

⊗ What It Isn't

Teaching without enthusiasm

Example: The teacher began a review of metric measurement concepts the fourth graders had learned. She stated, "Take out a piece of paper. Write your name at the top. I'm going to ask questions that require you to convert metric linear measurements to standard linear measurements. You can use the charts at the front of the room to help you. Ready? Number one: Ten centimeters equals approximately how many inches?" The teacher continued asking nineteen additional similar questions.

⊘ What It Is

Leading students to perceive the content being presented as relevant

Example: To introduce a unit about the causes of World War II, the teacher engaged students in a discussion about the economic difficulties of their community and how some political groups were quick to blame various demographic groups for their economic woes. Using newspaper websites, the students found quotes from various politicians who implicitly or explicitly blamed certain groups for the nation's or the community's economic difficulties. Then the teacher had students work in groups to read different speeches that Hitler gave in the early 1930s. The groups were asked to identify similarities and differences between Hitler's use of blame and the ways contemporary politicians use blame.

(X) What It Isn't

Assuming that students will perceive the relevance of the content being presented

> Example: To introduce a unit about the causes of World War II, the teacher presented a lecture on the rise of Hitler in Germany in the 1930s. The lecture described Hitler's skill at convincing the German people that their economic problems were due to the unfair practices of other European nations and the wealth of Jewish businessmen.

(✓) What It Is

Using project-based learning

> Students in a Spanish class were learning how they would engage in a dialogue with someone they just met. The teacher asked the students to first write their dialogue in Spanish on their iPads. Before submitting the written task to the teacher, students checked their dialogue with the rubric the teacher provided. Using the classroom's learning management system, the teacher quickly checked each student's written dialogue and gave students permission to proceed. Next, students used their iPads to record themselves speaking the dialogue. Students were encouraged to modify their voices so an audience could distinguish the participants in the dialogue. The new rubric emphasized correct pronunciation and speaking with expression. The audio recordings were sent to the teacher for the teacher's review. Finally, the teacher allowed students to bring their dialogue to life with an animated drawing program. At the end of the lesson, students had created a cartoon with a dialogue in Spanish.

(X) What It Isn't

Engaging in a project that doesn't advance the intended learning

> Students in a Spanish class were learning how they would engage in a dialogue with someone they just met. The teacher asked the students to first write their dialogue in Spanish. When students finished, they were allowed to construct a diorama featuring life in a pueblo.

✓ What It Is

Integrating the arts, technology, and physical education into core academic instruction

> Example: The elementary teachers were frustrated about the difficulties they encountered as they tried to guide students to learn multiplication facts. The physical education teacher (who participated in the planning meeting) decided that she could help. In the various games she organized for students, she decided to change the number of points associated with a score. For example, to help students practice counting by and multiplying by eight, the teacher announced that each soccer goal would earn eight points. As students scored, she required them to calculate their point total, counting by the appropriate number and reciting the associated multiplication fact. Students yelled, "Eight, sixteen, twenty-four, thirty-two. Eight times four equals thirty-two," as they scored for the fourth time.

✗ What It Isn't

Missing opportunities to integrate the arts, technology, and physical education into core academic instruction

> Example: The elementary teachers were frustrated about the difficulties they encountered as they tried to teach students multiplication facts. They decided they were doing all they could reasonably do, considering the importance of other math concepts and skills in the curriculum. They blamed the students' parents for not spending adequate time helping their children practice multiplication facts.

✓ What It Is

Promoting student-to-student interaction

> Example: A third-grade teacher introduced the idea that fractions can help describe the relationship between the number of objects within a set and the entire number of objects in the set. The teacher modeled the concept by projecting a photograph of seven students in her classroom. The teacher commented, "There are seven students in the picture and two are wearing jackets. So, two-sevenths of the students are wearing jackets." Then the teacher asked other students to describe fractions they observe in the photo. Several students suggested good answers, and the teacher decided that the class was ready for a cooperative learning activity. The teacher divided the students into five groups. She made sure that at least one of her most capable mathematicians was in each group. One student served as the group's recorder. Another served as the group's accuracy checker. She assigned two students in each group

to observe particularly what students in the pictures were wearing or their physical characteristics. Additionally, she asked two students to focus upon what students in the pictures were doing. When the teacher flashed a picture on the screen, each group was expected to work together to brainstorm and record as many accurate sentences as possible, describing fractions represented in the picture. They were required to do so before the timer rang. As soon as the first picture was displayed, Latoya (one of the students who was supposed to watch what students were wearing) gave her group an answer: "Two-fifths of the kids in the picture are wearing red shirts." "I don't get it," Jerome declared. "How many kids are in the picture?" Latoya asked. "I see five," answered Jerome, thinking maybe it was a trick question. "How many kids are wearing red shirts?" asked Latoya. "Two," Jerome answered with a little more confidence. "Right! Two-fifths of the kids are wearing red shirts. Two out of five," Latoya explained. "Oh, I get it!" Jerome blurted and then added, "Like, four-fifths are wearing socks." "Yes, write it down," Latoya directed, as the group tried to create more sentences.

Ⓧ What It Isn't

Missing opportunities to promote student-to-student interaction

Example: A third-grade teacher introduced the idea that fractions can help describe the relationship between the number of objects within a set and the entire number of objects in the set. Using a projector, she showed pictures of groups of students in the classroom. The teacher called upon individual students to create sentences that described a portion of the students in each snapshot. "Mark, what fraction do you see represented in this picture?" the teacher asked. When Mark did not respond, she called upon Adriana (who always has her hand raised). "Three-fifths of the students are wearing blue jeans," Adriana asserted correctly. "Yes," the teacher answered, relieved that someone got the answer right. "Who else sees a fraction represented in this picture?" The teacher ignored Latoya (another perennial hand-raiser) and called upon Jerome, but Jerome bit his lip and shrugged his shoulders. Then the teacher called upon Latoya. "Two-fifths of the kids in the picture are wearing red shirts," Latoya answered proudly. For the rest of the period, the teacher interacted with Adriana, Latoya, and two other students who seem to understand the concept. Other students sat quietly, seemingly attempting to figure out what all this meant.

Practice Guide Related to Leading Students to Love Learning

For information on possible uses of this practice guide, please see pages 5–6 in Chapter 1.

Table 8.1

1.	Did the teacher demonstrate enthusiasm for the content taught?	Ⓨ	Ⓝ
2.	Did the teacher demonstrate enthusiasm for the students learning the content?	Ⓨ	Ⓝ
3.	Was the lesson likely to generate student enthusiasm for the content?	Ⓨ	Ⓝ
4.	Did students understand the importance of the objective to their current or future real-life situations?	Ⓨ	Ⓝ
5.	Did the teacher encourage student-to-student conversation concerning the objective?	Ⓨ	Ⓝ
6.	Did the lesson include project-based components?	Ⓨ	Ⓝ
7.	Did the teacher integrate content from other disciplines in teaching the lesson objective?	Ⓨ	Ⓝ
8.	Did students use technology to help them learn the lesson objective?	Ⓨ	Ⓝ
9.	Did the teacher allow students to manipulate objects related to the lesson objective?	Ⓨ	Ⓝ
10.	Did the lesson lead students to a level of mastery or skill attainment higher than typical for students at the same grade level?	Ⓨ	Ⓝ

In a strong lesson, a "yes" answer is recorded for at least five of these items.
In an outstanding lesson, a "yes" answer is recorded for at least seven of these items.

Practical Next Steps 💡

1. In collaboration with teacher colleagues, engage in a book study of *Project-Based Teaching: How to Create Rigorous and Engaging Learning Experiences* (Boss & Larmer, 2018).

2. In collaboration with colleagues, ask yourselves what percentage of your students were highly excited about participating in the most recent lesson you completed. Consider the following as you think about strategies for making your next lesson more likely to result in your students loving the content you're teaching:

   a. List ways you could better demonstrate your enthusiasm for the learning objective.

   b. List ways you could better demonstrate your enthusiasm for your students understanding and mastering the learning objective.

   c. List ways you could help your students see the learning objective as relevant to their lives.

    d. List ways you could design the lesson to include the elements of project-based teaching in a way that is likely to help students achieve the learning objective.

    e. List ways you could integrate the arts, music, or technology into your teaching of the learning objective.

    f. List ways you could utilize cooperative learning or other student-to-student interactions as you pursue the learning objective.

    g. List ways you can design the lesson so students are likely to achieve a learning outcome that goes beyond what students at the grade level typically achieve.

    h. What supports can you integrate into the lesson that might help students achieve a rigorous learning outcome?

3. Interview four or five of your students about the last lesson you taught. Ask students to share what might have made the lesson more exciting or more relevant to them. Use their feedback to help plan a stronger lesson.

4. Invite a colleague to visit your classroom and offer feedback about how your lessons might be improved in a way that leads more students to love learning. After the colleague provides feedback, offer to visit your colleague's classroom, observe, and provide feedback.

References

Barron, B., & Darling-Hammond, L. (2008). How can we teach for meaningful learning? In L. Darling-Hammond (Ed.), *Powerful learning: What we know about teaching for understanding* (pp. 11–70). San Francisco, CA: Jossey-Bass.

Boss, S., & Larmer, J. (2018). *Project based teaching: How to create rigorous and engaging learning experiences.* Alexandria, VA: Association for Supervision and Curriculum Development.

Hattie, J. (2009). *Visible learning: A synthesis of over 800 meta-analyses relating to achievement.* New York, NY: Routledge.

Hug, B., Krajcik, J., & Marx, R. (2005). Using innovative learning technologies to promote learning and engagement in an urban science classroom. *Urban Education, 40*(4), 446–472.

Kensler, L., & Uline, C. L. (2017). *Leadership for Green Schools: Sustainability for our children, our communities, and our planet.* New York: Routledge and Taylor and Francis Group.

McCullen, C. (2003). Celebrating differences. *Principal Leadership, 3*(8), 34–36.

9 Developing Best Teaching Practices Throughout a School

Perhaps the most important lesson to be learned from our studies of high-performing urban schools is that success is attainable. Typical urban schools, with significant challenges, can achieve substantial improvements in teaching that yield remarkable gains in learning. This lesson is important, yet also fairly obvious. An equally important lesson is that achieving schoolwide improvements in teaching is difficult. This lesson remains elusive in part because, in these outstanding schools, teachers make their work appear easy or at least natural. As one watches teachers at Jim Thorpe Fundamental Academy in Santa Ana, California, involve students in gallery walks of their California Missions projects, one does not see the hundreds of hours of professional development and planning that supported teachers' efforts to improve student engagement. As an observer sees teachers at Trinidad Garza Early College High School in Dallas, Texas, prepare students to succeed in college-level courses, the months and years teachers spent coming to know their students, master their content, and establish a college-going culture within their school may not be readily apparent. As a visitor watches teachers at Lauderbach Elementary in Chula Vista, California, engage students in focused conversations, one might mistakenly think that teachers always taught with such an intense focus on specific objectives.

Generating consistent schoolwide change in teaching takes substantial time, effort, courage, and risk. In this chapter, we describe what we have learned about how urban schools generate equitable and excellent teaching practices. First, we start by discussing the goal of improvement efforts. If a school is to achieve outstanding results, there must be clarity about the goal and the elements that contribute to the goal. Second, we describe a system that can facilitate the attainment of the goal. After observing so many high-performing urban schools and interviewing hundreds of principals, district administrators, support personnel, teachers, and students, we have learned that schoolwide improvement requires a carefully orchestrated system. Based on our studies, we propose a coherent educational improvement system that reflects the best practices of many high-performing urban schools. Many of these ideas are discussed in greater detail in *Leadership in America's Best Urban Schools* (Johnson, Uline, & Perez; 2015); however, this brief overview is intended to support educators who wish to begin planning how they might increase equity and excellence in their schools.

A Perpetual Question

On the Minds of Educators Striving to Produce Equity and Excellence

How can I get each and every one of my colleagues to think, "How can we work together to generate outstanding learning results for each and every one of our students?"

Pursuing the Right Goal

Educator and author Lawrence Peter said, "If you don't know where you are going, you will probably end up somewhere else." If we don't have clarity about what we want to achieve, our chances of success are diminished. While such clarity sometimes eludes individuals, it can be even more difficult for groups (such as teams of educators) to acquire and maintain.

Most educators want their schools to be better; however, there are vastly different notions about what "better" means. Some educators hope to be part of a school where high-achieving students are more likely to excel in phenomenal ways. Some educators simply aspire to work in a safer, calmer environment. Others believe that their school would be better if they offered a particular type of program or curricular innovation. In the high-performing urban schools we studied, the overarching goal was *outstanding academic achievement for each and every student*. Leaders (including school administrators, teacher leaders, and sometimes district leaders) wanted to create learning environments where all students would succeed academically, personally, and socially. They committed themselves to pursuing both excellence and equity while rejecting the notion that schools would inevitably create winners and losers (Blankstein & Noguera, 2015).

If you and your colleagues are committed to promoting excellence and equity at your school, it is critical that you begin developing strong, common mental images of what this goal implies. What would excellence and equity look like at your school? What would be different if you were leading every student toward the attainment of impressive learning results? As you consider these questions, it is important to keep in mind that we found three tightly related characteristics in the high-performing urban schools we studied: a positive transformational culture for all students and all adults at the school, access to challenging curricula for all students, and effective, engaging instruction that leads all students to understanding and mastery. These empowering characteristics are illustrated in Figure 9.1 in a manner intended to convey that they are interrelated. Also, the illustration is intended to highlight our finding that a positive transformational culture is the foundation for improvement efforts.

Positive Transformational Culture

As described by Johnson et al. (2015), the high-performing schools we studied:

. . . established a positive transformational culture that made the school a place where all students (regardless of race/ethnicity, family income, language background, gender, sexual orientation, disability status, or other demographic group) were eager to come to school, learn and grow As well,

Figure 9.1

the school became a place where adults (teachers, support staff, volunteers, and administrators) were eager to come to work, learn, and grow as members of a team that made an increasingly powerful difference in the lives of students.

(p. 20)

Without a positive transformational culture, other improvement efforts are built on quicksand. If certain groups of students do not perceive that they are welcome, appreciated, respected, and valued, they will not engage in ways that are essential to the attainment of equitable and excellent learning results. If certain groups of adult stakeholders do not perceive that they are welcome, appreciated, respected, and valued, they too will not engage in ways that are crucial to the school's success. If teachers feel that nobody notices their efforts to try, they are less likely to keep trying. Efforts to pursue schoolwide implementation of any of the teaching practices described in this book will not generate the desired impact if there is not a strong, positive transformational culture for both students and adults.

It is important to note that we label the culture as "transformational" to reflect our finding that educators cared deeply enough to be willing to transform their practices in ways that would ensure the success of all students. In many schools, educators care, but perhaps not enough to engage in the work necessary to transform practices, routines, and structures to which they have become accustomed.

Access to Challenging Curricula for All Students

As reflected in many of the teaching practices described in this book, educators in the high-performing urban schools we studied sought to give all students access to challenging curricula. Educators envisioned a school where all students, including (among others) students whose first language was not English, students who were performing two or three years below grade level when they first enrolled, students with learning disabilities, and students in foster care had outstanding opportunities to learn challenging academic curricula. While a positive transformational culture formed the foundation for improvement efforts, educators recognized that the provision of access to rich, balanced, challenging curricula was essential to the construction of learning environments that generated both equity and excellence.

As educators considered what they would teach, they recognized there would never be sufficient time to teach their students everything they wanted students to know. Educators rejected the notion of "mile-wide, inch-deep" curricula and instead focused on the rigorous standards they believed were most important to their students' current and future educational success.

Educators planned what Marzano (2003) defined as a guaranteed and viable curriculum. Educators determined what academic goals were important enough to guarantee that all students would have real opportunities to learn. The guarantee implied that all students would have a high likelihood of learning the content whether they took seventh-grade science from Mrs. Smith or Mr. Garcia, whether they were placed in the general English section or the honors English class, whether or not they received special education services, and whether they received instruction primarily in Spanish or English. As well, educators planned to ensure that the curriculum was viable, such that there was adequate time for all students to understand and master the guaranteed learning goals. Educators in the high-performing schools knew that learning goals were not viable if teachers barely had time to cover the content and ensure that their students understood and mastered the content.

Effective, Engaging Instruction That Leads All Students to Understanding and Mastery

While challenging curricula defined what students were expected to learn in high-performing urban schools, effective, engaging instruction defined how instruction was expected to facilitate learning for all students. Educators recognized that instruction would not be effective (generate desired learning results) for students who were not engaged. Thus, educators committed themselves to improving instruction in ways that engaged every student in learning important concepts and skills. As well, educators understood that many traditional teaching practices had limited evidence of effectiveness for the diverse populations of they served. This book provides considerable information about the teaching practices used in high-performing urban schools to ensure all students would understand and master the guaranteed and viable curriculum educators established.

Any team of educators committed to pursuing equitable, excellent learning results for all students should spend time envisioning a positive, transformational culture, access to challenging curricula, and the establishment of effective, engaging instruction for all students. Educators should consider what these three characteristics would look like at their schools. What would need to change? What might stay the same? Establishing a shared vision of the goal is an important first step on the journey to achieving great learning results for all students.

Building a Coherent Education Improvement System

Individuals may sincerely want to change their practices; however, systems are often not designed to support the desired changes. In some cases, systems may work in ways that frustrate change efforts. In the high-performing schools we studied, systems were developed in ways that led to five outcomes. These outcomes, illustrated in Figure 9.2, supported educators' efforts to establish positive transformational cultures, ensure access to challenging academic curricula, and provide effective, engaging instruction for all students.

Focus on Specific Concepts and Skills

First, educators recognized the need to work toward common understandings of what they would expect themselves to teach their students. If they were to offer a guaranteed and viable curriculum, educators needed to agree upon the learning expectations associated with grade levels and subject areas. They had to decide which standards every student would learn and which ones would have lower priority. They had to decide and agree upon what each standard meant and what each standard implied students should know and be able to do. Furthermore, they had to agree how they would coordinate across grade levels and course sequences to ensure

Figure 9.2

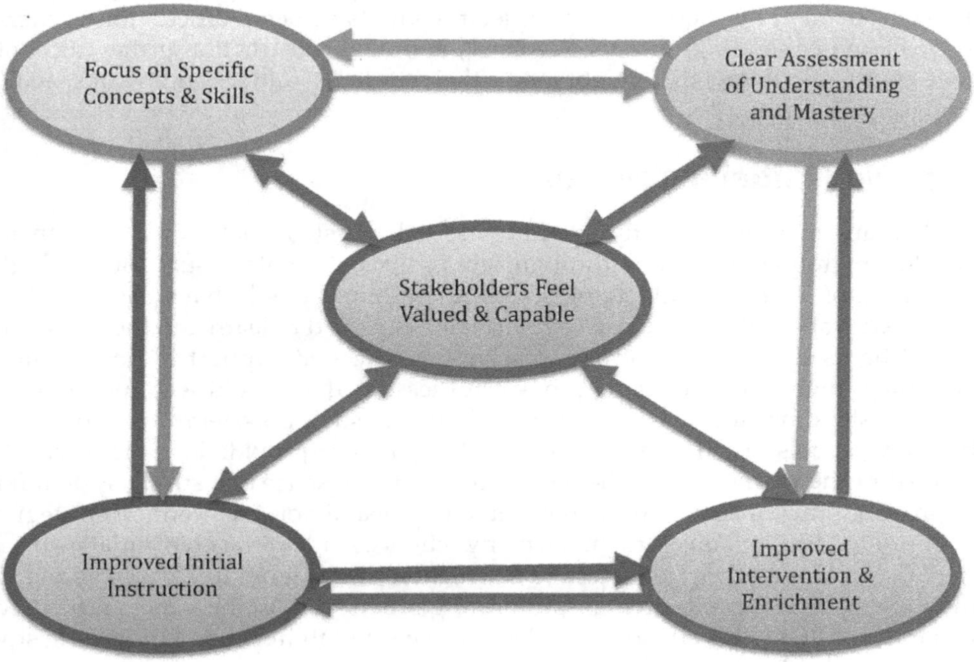

that students would have a logical path to the attainment of the specific concepts and skills. The system had to be structured in a way that helped educators establish a common focus on specific concepts and skills. As well, the system needed to work in ways that continuously refined the focus so educators became increasingly clear about what they needed to help their students learn. In the absence of such a system, it would have been difficult for teachers to develop and sustain many of the teaching practices described in this book. As well, student access to challenging academic curricula would have been severely limited.

Clear Assessment of Understanding and Mastery

Once educators in high-performing schools began to establish clarity about what they wanted their students to learn, they needed to develop clear, common understandings of how they would assess understanding and mastery. They needed agreement about what mastery looked like for students at the grade levels they taught. They needed to determine what they would accept as evidence that their students had developed deep understandings of concepts and skills. The system needed to yield common formative assessments that teachers would use at approximately the same time. The formative assessments needed to provide students and teachers useful information about the depth of a student's understanding of a specific concept rather than a general sense of a student's understanding of a variety of concepts (DuFour & Marzano, 2011). Additionally, the system needed to help teachers develop even more immediate ways of determining what students understood. Teachers needed multiple strategies for gauging student progress and rapidly adjusting instruction. In the absence of such support, it is difficult to imagine teachers experiencing a high level of success implementing the teaching practices described in this book. For example, it would have been difficult for teachers to check understanding, provide feedback, and adapt instruction if they did not have clarity about how they might assess their students' understanding of specific academic concepts.

Improved Initial Instruction

Perhaps most importantly, teachers needed a system that would help them develop high-quality lessons through which their students would have a high likelihood of learning challenging standards. While it would have been great to have clarity about the standards students were expected to learn and the tools that would be used to assess learning, teachers still needed support in determining how they might create engaging, powerful lessons that would lead all students to understanding and mastery. In many schools, such a system does not exist. In many schools, teachers are limited to the guidance provided by the teacher's manual or the worksheets in the file cabinet. In the absence of a strong system for improving initial instruction, schools must rely heavily on intervention strategies to improve learning outcomes. In too many schools, students receive initial instruction, fail, and only then get access to instruction that is more likely to respond to their strengths and needs. In high-performing urban schools, the system is focused in a manner that helps ensure initial lessons have a high likelihood of leading students to understanding and mastery.

Improved Intervention and Enrichment

Even with improved initial instruction, there will always be some students who need additional support. In high-performing urban schools, the system is designed to promptly identify students who need extra support and intervention, provide support in an efficient and highly effective manner, and continuously improve the quality of intervention efforts. As well, because there will always be some students who achieve understanding and mastery more quickly than anticipated, it is important for the system to ensure the provision of enrichment in ways that build upon student strengths and maximize student interest in learning.

Stakeholders Feel Valued and Capable

If schools are to succeed in creating positive transformational cultures, all of the previously described system outcomes must be pursued in a manner that results in all stakeholders feeling valued and capable. For example, if the pursuit of improved initial instruction occurs in a manner that leaves teachers feeling punished and humiliated, the effort is not likely to produce the intended result. Similarly, if intervention strategies are constructed in a way that leaves students feeling punished and humiliated, the efforts will not be effective. A positive transformational culture is central to any sustained improvement effort. Therefore, all of the system outcomes must be pursued in a manner that leads stakeholders to feel valued and capable.

System Elements

In high-performing urban schools we studied, leaders were focused on pursuing the five outcomes described above. To move toward those outcomes, they designed, strengthened, modified, and aligned several key system elements. Most commonly, they addressed the following five elements: teacher collaboration, professional development, classroom observation and feedback, schedules, and progress monitoring.

Teacher collaboration was a powerful engine of change in the high-performing urban schools we studied. Many aspects of the teacher collaboration we observed were consistent with the concept of professional learning communities. In fact, the five outcomes described above align (at least in part) to the three critical questions that drive the efforts of professional learning communities (DuFour, DuFour, Eaker, & Karhanek, 2004):

1. What is it we want all students to learn—by grade level, by course, and by unit of instruction?

2. How will we know when each student has acquired the intended knowledge and skills?

3. How will we respond when students experience initial difficulty so that we can improve upon current levels of learning?

(p. 2–3)

The first question aligns precisely with the outcome: Focus on Specific Concepts and Skills. The second question is consistent with the outcome: Clear Assessment of Understanding and Mastery. The third question is parallel to the outcome: Improved Intervention and Enrichment. As well, however, we believe the work of professional learning communities aligns with the outcome: Improved Initial Instruction. Also, we believe the spirit of professional learning communities is consistent with the outcome: Stakeholders Feel Valued and Capable.

Through regular, intensive, and focused teacher collaboration, educators, throughout almost all of the 150 schools we awarded, accelerated their progress toward positive, transformational cultures, challenging academic curricula, and effective, engaging instruction for all students. In collaboration meetings, teachers determined what they wanted their students to learn, how they would determine if their students achieved mastery, and how they would provide clear, engaging, culturally, socially, and personally responsive lessons. As well, through collaboration, teachers determined how they would check understanding, provide feedback, and adapt instruction. When they reviewed learning data, collaboration teams determined which students needed intervention and enrichment. As well, they determined what intervention or enrichment would be most effective and how they would evaluate the success of those efforts. Consistently, teachers credited their collaboration teams with helping them improve their teaching practices. It is difficult to envision a school achieving excellent and equitable learning results without strong teacher collaboration wherein teachers persistently ask themselves, "How will we plan and deliver quality-first instruction that leads nearly all students to mastery?"

Professional development was also an important system element that influenced change in high-performing urban schools. Often, professional development was tailored to needs teachers identified in their collaboration teams. At times, professional development was provided by district personnel or outside experts; however, teachers often provided professional development to peers at their own school. By sharing data and discussing practices in collaboration meetings, educators became aware of best practices within their schools and called upon their resident experts to help them improve teaching and learning.

It is also important to note that professional development was neither random nor episodic. Educators tended to focus on just a few topics each year, and they gave themselves opportunities to learn in depth. Educators were committed to ensuring that the concepts they learned through professional development would be practiced, refined, and implemented well. For example, at Lawndale High School near Los Angeles, California, leaders told us that they had been working on checking for understanding for the past two years. Almost all of their professional development efforts had been focused on improving their practice related to this issue.

In many high-performing urban schools, professional development did not resemble traditional in-service activities. For example, in some schools, a powerful professional development was a field trip (for the educators) to a high-performing urban school. In other schools, like MacArthur High School in Houston, the teachers' bus trip through their students' neighborhoods might have been more impactful than any traditional training experience. Whether traditional or unique, professional development was tailored to achieve the five outcomes described above.

Classroom observation and feedback was another important system element used in pursuit of the system outcomes described earlier. Principals spent a substantial amount of time observing instruction and providing teachers constructive feedback that helped them improve teaching practices. Typically, leaders focused their observations and feedback on a small number of key concerns, often informed by previous professional development efforts. By doing so, leaders helped teachers improve student learning outcomes over time.

While the quantity of observation and feedback in high-performing urban schools generally surpassed that found in struggling urban schools, the spirit behind observation and feedback probably held more importance than the quantity. In high-performing urban schools, teachers reported that their leaders wanted them to succeed. Observation and feedback were designed to help educators successfully reach and teach their students. To ensure that observation and feedback occurred in a manner that helped stakeholders feel valued and capable, leaders developed and maintained high levels of trust.

As emphasized by Theokas, Gonzalez, Manriquez, and Johnson (2019), principals in high-performing urban schools distributed leadership in ways that engaged many others in supporting efforts to improve teaching and learning. As a result, in many schools, teacher leaders and other school administrators participated in efforts to observe, support, and offer useful feedback.

A fourth important system element was the school schedule. Scheduling regular time for teacher collaboration was critical to the success of high-performing schools we studied. As well, at many schools, educators spent considerable time designing schedules that ensured all students access to a rich, balanced curriculum. Leaders worked diligently to plan schedules in ways that provided students access to dual-enrollment courses, Advanced Placement courses, and other enriching learning opportunities. Without careful attention to scheduling, it would have been difficult for many high-performing schools to implement changes in culture, curricula, and instruction.

Finally, we found that progress monitoring was an important system element in the high-performing urban schools. Schools developed and implemented strategies for monitoring the progress of individual students toward important learning goals. A focus on the success of each and every student could not have been established and sustained without specific, well-organized strategies for collecting, analyzing, and responding to student data. While individual schools might have utilized other system elements, these five were most important in generating improved learning results in high-performing urban schools.

In sum, one should remember that many schools have some type of teacher collaboration, almost all have some quantity of professional development, and classroom observation and feedback occur even in the most dismal schools. In addition, most schools rely upon a schedule or a master schedule, and progress monitoring is by no means exclusive to high-performing schools. These system elements were powerful in high-performing urban schools, because they were focused squarely on achieving the outcomes described earlier.

Summary

It should be noted that in high-performing urban schools, the five elements described above were aligned in ways that consistently emphasized and supported the same desired teaching practices. For example, we found the same teaching practices addressed in both professional development activities and in teacher collaboration meetings. Teachers planned together to implement these practices well in initial instruction, intervention, and enrichment activities. Additionally, we found that classroom observations and feedback were often focused upon the same practices. Such alignment helped increase the likelihood that teachers would successfully implement important teaching practices. Through the alignment of professional development, teacher collaboration, and classroom observation and feedback, teachers knew how their teaching practices could be improved. Additionally, teachers knew they enjoyed abundant support from their colleagues and leaders as they attempted to implement improvements.

References

Blankstein, A. M., & Noguera, P. (2015). *Excellence through equity: Five principles of courageous leadership to guide achievement for every student.* Thousand Oaks, CA: Corwin.

DuFour, R., DuFour, R., Eaker, R., & Karhanek, G. (2004). *Whatever it takes: How professional learning communities respond when kids don't learn.* Bloomington, IN: Solution Tree Press.

Dufour, R., & Marzano, R. J. (2011). *Leaders of learning: How district, school, and classroom leaders improve student achievement.* Bloomington, IN: Solution Tree Press.

Johnson, J. F., Uline, C. L., & Perez, L. G. (2015). *Leadership in America's best urban schools.* New York: Routledge and Taylor and Francis Group.

Marzano, R. J. (2003). *What works in schools: Translating research into action.* Alexandria, VA: Association for Supervision and Curriculum Development.

Theokas, C., Gonzalez, M. L., Manriquez, C., & Johnson, J. F. (2019). *Five practices for improving the success of Latino students: A guide for secondary school leaders.* New York: Routledge and Taylor and Francis Group.

Conclusion

Mathematicians relish the notion of existence proofs. If they can find just one example that contradicts a theorem, the existence of the one example proves the theorem inaccurate. The schools we have discussed in this book are existence proofs. They prove false the notion that urban schools serving low-income communities are doomed to low levels of academic achievement.

In this book, we have attempted to capture and describe the salient characteristics of instruction in high-performing urban schools. We have struggled to do so in a manner that adequately credits the impressive efforts of educators at these schools. Nonetheless, we encourage our readers to see for themselves. Visit these or similar schools, observe their classrooms, talk with their teachers, watch their planning meetings, listen to their problem-solving discussions, and see how they interact with students. Work to build upon our descriptions of their teaching practices in ways that add texture, depth, and meaning.

It is also important to note that while instruction is particularly important at these schools, there are many other important elements at play. For example, within these schools, we see many powerful practices that influence school climate and culture. Educators at these schools are impressively adept at creating environments in which students, parents, and other educators feel respected, valued, and appreciated. While this book touched upon some of these issues, there is much more to share that falls beyond the scope of this book.

Similarly, it is important to note that leadership in these schools is a critical topic. While leadership is discussed tangentially throughout the book and more directly in Chapter 9, there is much more to be said about the role leaders play in initiating and sustaining change efforts in high-performing urban schools.

If these high-performing schools stand as existence proofs, then we should share a renewed sense of urgency. These schools prove to us that, as a nation, we can do better for our children. Opportunity gaps and achievement gaps need not exist. As educators, we have the power to positively influence students' lives.

Appendix A
America's Best Urban Schools Award 2020 Eligibility Criteria

The America's Best Urban Schools Award (ABUS) is presented annually to the nation's highest-performing urban schools. In May 2020, the National Center for Urban School Transformation (NCUST) will present this award to elementary schools, middle schools, high schools, dual-language schools, and alternative schools. In order to compete for an America's Best Urban Schools Award, schools must submit the following data and meet or exceed the criteria as defined.

1. **Urban Location:** The school must be located in a metropolitan area with 50,000 or more residents.

2. **Non-Selective Admissions:** In general, the school may not require students to meet academic criteria in order to attain or retain admission. For example, a school that requires students to possess/maintain a certain test score or possess/maintain a minimum grade point average would not be eligible for consideration. Schools may house programs (e.g., programs for students identified as gifted or talented) that admit children from beyond the school's attendance area through selective admissions if fewer than 10 percent of the school's students are enrolled through selective admissions.

3. **Low-Income Eligibility:** For elementary schools in which the highest grade is grade six or lower, at least 60% of the students enrolled (both in the prior and the current year) must have met eligibility criteria for free-or reduced-price lunch. For middle schools (grade nine or lower), at least 50% of the students must have met the same criteria. In high schools, at least 40% of the students must have met the same criteria.

4. **High Rates of Academic Proficiency:** The school must be able to show that the percentage of students demonstrating proficiency on state assessments, in both 2018 and 2019, was higher than the average of all schools in the state (within the same grade span grouping). The school must have exceeded the state average in at least half of the subject areas/grade levels assessed in 2018 and 2019. NOTE: In states where rates of academic proficiency are not being tabulated in 2019 because of new assessments, NCUST will use 2017 and 2018 data to assess this criterion. In states where rates of academic proficiency were not tabulated in 2018 because of new assessments,

NCUST will use 2019 assessment data only. This note applies to items 4 through 7.

5. **High Rates of Academic Proficiency for Every Racial/Ethnic Group:** The school must indicate the percentage of students from each racial/ethnic group who achieved academic proficiency. The school may be eligible to compete only if, in at least two academic subjects, the percentage of students proficient in each racial/ethnic group exceeds the average of all schools in the state.

6. **Evidence of High Achievement for English Learners:** If more than 20 students are identified as English learners, the school must present evidence that a high percentage of English learners are progressing toward proficiency with the English language. As well, the school must indicate the percentage of English learners that achieved proficiency on state assessments.

7. **Evidence of High Achievement for Students with Disabilities:** The school must indicate the percentage of students with disabilities that achieved proficiency on state assessments.

8. **Low Rates of Out-of-School Suspension:** For every demographic group served, with an enrollment greater than 20, the total number of student days lost to suspensions must be less than the total number of students enrolled.

9. **High Attendance Rates:** The school must have evidence to indicate that the average student attendance rate exceeded 92% for each of the past two academic years.

10. **Low Rates of Teacher Absence:** Schools must indicate the percentage of teachers who were absent more than 10 days.

11. Schools must also respond to several open-ended questions that ask for evidence of rigorous curricula, engaging and effective instruction, a positive school culture, student engagement in extracurricular activities, excellence in Science, Technology, Engineering, and Mathematics education (STEM) and describe what efforts the school is making to ensure students are successful in subsequent school levels (e.g. elementary schools must show evidence that their students are successful at the middle school).

Additional Criteria for High Schools

In addition to the general criteria, high schools must meet the following criteria:

12. **Percentage of First-Year High School Students Advancing to the Second Year:** Each high school must present the number and percentage of their 2018–2019 first-year students who earned sufficient credit to be promoted to second-year status.

13. **Percentage of Students Earning College Credit or Participating in Advanced Placement Courses during High School:** Each school must present evidence of the number and percentage of students who earned college credit in the prior year. Also, each applicant must present evidence of the number and percentage of students who participated in advanced placement or international baccalaureate courses; the number and percentage who took advanced placement or international baccalaureate assessments; and the number and percentage who received passing scores. Schools also provide average SAT/ACT scores.

14. **High Graduation Rates:** Each high school must present the latest four-year adjusted cohort graduation rate (as defined by the U.S. Department of Education) for every racial/ethnic group of students.

Additional Criteria for Dual Language Schools

In addition to the general criteria, dual language schools must meet the following criteria:

15. **Schools that apply in the dual language category must provide school-wide dual language programs.** Dual language applicants must meet all other award criteria.

Additional Criteria for Alternative Schools

In addition to the general criteria, alternative schools must meet the following criteria:

16. **Alternative school applicants must meet criteria one through three above.** Regarding item two, alternative schools may be considered if they selectively enroll students who have experienced academic and behavioral difficulty in typical schools. Additionally, alternative schools must present data regarding all other criteria (4 through 15); however, there are not minimal eligibility criteria associated with these criteria. Alternative schools will be reviewed and considered on a competitive basis.

Reproduced with permission from The National Center for Urban School Transformation

Appendix B
About the Schools Awarded and Studied

The schools NCUST awarded and studied varied in many ways. For example, the size of the awarded schools varied. Some of the awarded schools are small, serving only 100 to 400 students. The smaller schools included charter schools, career pathway high schools, and small neighborhood schools. In contrast, NCUST also awarded large elementary and middle schools serving 1,000 to 1,800 students. In addition, NCUST has awarded some large comprehensive high schools serving more than 2,000 students. School size has never been a selection criterion. Instead, NCUST has been open to the possibility that schools can create equitable and excellent learning opportunities, regardless of the size of the student population.

In addition, the schools varied in grade configurations. The majority of schools awarded have been elementary schools; however, NCUST has awarded elementary, middle, and high schools with varying grade configurations. Even though schools presented different challenges, programs, and practices, all of the schools presented strong evidence that they were achieving excellent and equitable learning results.

In order to apply for the award, schools had to demonstrate that they served large percentages of students who typically were not served well in public schools. First, given our Center's mission, the schools had to be situated in urban areas. Minimally, the school had to be in an area designated by the U.S. Census Bureau as a metropolitan statistical area. These areas have populations of at least 50,000 residents. This broad definition allowed us to consider schools that were in inner-ring suburbs such as Maplewood, Missouri (next to St. Louis) or Revere, Massachusetts (next to Boston). As well, award winners have included many schools in typical big-city urban districts such as the New York City Public Schools, Chicago Public Schools, the Houston Independent School District, the Los Angeles Unified School District, the Miami-Dade Public Schools, the Cleveland Metropolitan School District, and the Metropolitan Nashville Public Schools.

Some might think that this book does not apply to their school or district, because they are not located within an "urban" area. While the schools discussed in this book all met the urban criteria described above, urbanicity is only one of the challenges these schools had to overcome. The book is about schools that overcame a variety of challenges to achieve educational excellence and equity. The book should be considered a resource to any educator who is committed to the pursuit of outstanding learning results for every demographic group of students they serve.

To ensure that applicant schools were grappling with and overcoming the real challenges associated with educating typical urban students, applicants were required to guarantee they did not use admission policies that allowed them to select students with better academic records or potential, or to reject students with fewer academic qualifications. NCUST disqualified schools that required students to take entrance tests or maintain certain grade-point averages. Magnet schools or charter schools could apply only if they accepted students on a first-come, first-served basis or if they used lotteries and/or attendance areas to determine which students would be enrolled. Of course, this restriction eliminated many outstanding schools from our consideration. However, by excluding schools with selective admission policies, we helped ensure that the schools we identified were achieving atypical learning results for typical urban students.

The majority of schools awarded have been typical public schools that serve students who live in the neighborhood surrounding the school; however, approximately 11 percent of the schools awarded have been charter schools. To identify schools that truly achieved excellence and equity, NCUST sought to ensure that students were not denied enrollment on the basis of academic performance.

It is also important to note that applicants had to serve predominantly low-income communities. In elementary schools, at least 60 percent of the students had to qualify for the federal free or reduced-price meal program. Often students in secondary schools are reluctant to apply for free-meal programs (even though they may not be more affluent than their siblings in elementary school). Consequently, we considered middle schools if at least 50 percent of the students met the low-income criteria, and we considered high schools if at least 40 percent of the students met low-income criteria. Even with these lenient criteria, in most of the schools NCUST awarded, over 75 percent of the students served met the family income criteria for the federal free or reduced-price meal program.

School Effectiveness Criteria

Applicants for the America's Best Urban Schools Award were required to meet multiple criteria related to excellence and equity (not just good test scores). For example, NCUST looked carefully at attendance rates, graduation rates, participation in advanced courses of study, suspension/expulsion rates, college entrance exam scores, and a variety of other indicators. For many indicators, applicants had to present data for the entire school population served, as well as data for each demographic group served. Applicants had to show that they maintained average daily attendance rates of at least 92 percent. They had to demonstrate very low suspension rates for all students and for every demographic group they served. High schools had to demonstrate strong graduation rates for all students and for every demographic group they served.

Results from state standardized tests were a critical determinant for many schools. Applicants were required to demonstrate that a higher percentage of their students achieved proficient or advanced academic levels than the statewide percentage of students who achieved proficient or advanced levels. On at least half of the tests administered for state accountability purposes, the school had to perform at or above the state average for two consecutive years.

Additionally, schools were required to show evidence of strong academic accomplishment for every racial/ethnic group of students they served. For each demographic group served, the school was required to demonstrate that the percentage of students performing at the proficient or advanced level was equal to or higher than the statewide percentage of all students who performed at those levels. Schools were required to demonstrate this high level of achievement on at least two state assessments. Please note that NCUST compared each demographic group to the statewide performance of all students, not simply the statewide performance of students in the same demographic group. This requirement eliminated many schools from consideration. For example, in some schools, Latino students performed very well compared to the average for other Latino students in the state; however, these schools would be considered for the America's Best Urban School Award only if Latino students (and every other racial/ethnic group served) achieved at a level higher than the average for *all* students in the state.

NCUST also required applicants to present strong evidence of academic success for students with emerging bilingualism and students with disabilities. Applicants had to demonstrate that students with emerging bilingualism were developing greater proficiency in the use of the English language as well as greater proficiency in academic areas. Schools also had to show data related to the academic progress of students with disabilities. In several winning schools, such as Mary Walke Stephens Elementary in Houston's Aldine Independent School District or Cerritos Elementary in the Glendale Unified School District in California, the percentage of students with emerging bilingualism who achieved proficiency on state assessments exceeded the overall statewide percentage of students who achieved proficiency. In sum, in order to qualify for the America's Best Urban School Award, schools were required to demonstrate evidence of academic excellence for every demographic group they served.

The Selection Process

Each year, many schools make inquiry about the America's Best Urban Schools Award. School and district personnel call with questions regarding the award criteria or attend the Center's free webinars regarding the application process. Often, these interactions result in school leaders determining that they do not qualify for the award program. Typically, applicants include fifty to eighty elementary, middle, and high schools. Applicants have included many National Blue Ribbon Schools, National Title I Distinguished Schools, schools recognized on *U.S. News & World Report's Best High Schools in America*, and schools that earned a wide array of statewide distinctions.

In order to apply, schools completed an application. Most of the application information focused upon quantitative data related to the award criteria (e.g., percentages of students meeting low-income criteria, average daily attendance percentages, percentages of students who performed at the proficient or advanced levels on state assessments, graduation rates, suspension rates, numbers of students in advanced classes). The applications provided schools limited opportunities to write narrative descriptions of their schools. By limiting the writing required, NCUST hoped to minimize the time school leaders had to spend preparing the application. As well, NCUST hoped to focus eligibility primarily on results achieved for diverse populations of students.

In addition to submitting an application, schools submitted a DVD with video recordings of two lessons. Schools were required to send video clips (between 10 and 30 minutes in length) featuring some of their best examples of instruction. The video recordings provided additional perspective on curricular rigor, instructional effectiveness, and the climate and culture of the school.

After reviewing the applications, NCUST selected as finalists the schools that presented the strongest evidence of academic success for all demographic groups of students. Schools that met all eligibility criteria but were not selected as finalists were listed on the Center's website as honor roll schools.

We conducted on-site visits to every finalist school. Teams of researchers, teachers, and administrators (including educators from previous winning schools) visited each finalist. Team members spent considerable amounts of time observing classrooms; interviewing teachers, administrators, counselors, students, and parents; and reviewing student work. With the permission of the interviewees, team members made audio recordings of the interviews and video recordings of some of the administrator interviews. Additionally, the teams observed teacher planning meetings, parent meetings, and staff meetings. They talked with district administrators and neighborhood leaders.

During our site visits, we noted evidence of the pursuit of excellent and equitable learning results beyond the impressive application data the schools submitted. For example, we noted that school personnel structured programs and services to ensure that students with emerging bilingualism were being taught the same challenging academic content provided to native English speakers. We found that assignments required students to think deeply about academic standards in ways that required the application of higher-order thinking skills. We observed teacher collaboration teams pushing themselves to design lessons that would intrigue and engage Black, Latino, and low-income students. We watched special education personnel work in general education classrooms to help ensure that students with disabilities progressed toward mastering the same academic standards all other students learned. We heard students from low-income families describe the many ways that teachers and administrators had helped them feel accepted, respected, and valued. As well, students shared how their relationships with school personnel positively influenced their motivation to work hard and excel.

By visiting and observing all classrooms in each finalist school, we affirmed that all students (regardless of demographic groups) were receiving access to challenging academic standards. By interviewing students and parents, we learned that the schools had developed cultures that helped all students believe that they had the opportunity to graduate, pursue postsecondary education, and succeed in meaningful careers. By interviewing large samples of teachers and administrators, we acquired evidence that educators were relentlessly striving to create learning conditions that ensured the success of all students and every demographic group of students they served. Equity and excellence were not merely slogans, random workshop topics, or bullet points buried within planning documents. Instead, the pursuit of excellent and equitable learning results was the underlying purpose for practically every activity, program, routine, and policy.

Over the past twelve years, NCUST refined observation and interview protocols so that we might learn more about the practices that influenced excellent and equitable learning results in high-performing urban schools. We endeavored to probe deeper to understand how leaders initiated changes, generated stakeholder commitment, managed setbacks, and sustained momentum.

Each year, after all site visits were completed, team leaders met to compare detailed notes from visits. The schools selected as award winners were those where team members found the most evidence of curricular rigor, instructional effectiveness, positive relationships, and focus on continuous improvement.

Additionally, apart from our award program, we conducted phone interviews and face-to-face interviews with selected teachers and administrators from these impressive schools. Our doctoral students engaged in in-depth case studies of several of the winning schools. We continue to examine data, identify themes, discuss conclusions, seek additional evidence, and deepen our understandings. These efforts continue to focus on developing deeper understandings of the factors that contribute to excellence and equity in these schools.

Appendix C
America's Best Urban Schools Award Winners

Alabama

- **Birmingham City Schools** (Birmingham, AL)
  Glen Iris Elementary (2013)
- **Dothan City Schools** (Dothan, AL)
  Morris Slingluff Elementary (2013)

Arizona

- **Phoenix Elementary School District** (Phoenix, AZ)
  Magnet Traditional School (2013)
- **Tucson Unified** (Tucson, AZ)
  C.E. Rose Elementary (2012)

California

- **Bakersfield City School District** (Bakersfield, CA):
  Franklin Elementary School (2008)
- **Baldwin Park Unified School District** (Baldwin Park, CA):
  Kenmore Elementary (2018)
- **Centinela Valley High School District** (Lawndale, CA—Los Angeles)
  Lawndale High School (2009)
- **Chula Vista ESD** (Chula Vista, CA):
  Feaster Charter School (2015)
  Myrtle S. Finney Elementary (2016)
  Hilltop Drive Elementary (2016)
  Lauderbach Elementary, (2012 & 2016)

Montgomery Elementary (2012)

Mueller Charter (2012)

Otay Elementary (2012)

◆ **Compton Unified School District** (Compton, CA)

Bursch Elementary (2009)

◆ **Cucamonga School District** (Rancho Cucamonga, CA—San Bernardino)

Rancho Cucamonga Middle School (2007)

◆ **Excellence and Justice in Education Academy** (El Cajon, CA)

Excellence and Justice in Education Academy

◆ **Garden Grove Unified School District** (Garden Grove, CA)

John A. Murdy School (2015)

◆ **Glendale Unified School District** (Glendale, CA)

Cerritos Elementary (2015)

Columbus Elementary (2012)

Horace Mann Elementary (2010 & 2016)

◆ **KIPP Charter** (San Diego, CA)

KIPP Adelante Academy (2009)

◆ **Long Beach Unified School District** (Long Beach, CA)

Thomas Edison Elementary (2007)

International Elementary (2010)

Keller Dual Immersion Middle School (2018)

Signal Hill Elementary (2008)

Tucker Elementary (2008)

◆ **Los Angeles Unified School District** (Los Angeles, CA)

Lemay Elementary (2010)

Nueva Vista Elementary (2010)

Synergy Charter Academy (2013)

◆ **Montebello Unified School District** (Montebello, CA—Los Angeles)

Montebello Gardens Elementary (2009)

◆ **National School District** (National City, CA—San Diego)

Ira Harbison School (2009)

◆ **Sacramento City Unified School District** (Sacramento, CA)
Golden Hill Elementary (2009)

◆ **San Diego Unified School District** (San Diego, CA)
Kearny High School of International Business (2009)
The O'Farrell Charter School (2015)

◆ **Santa Ana Unified** (Santa Ana, CA)
El Sol Science and Arts Academy (2017)
Jim Thorpe Fundamental Academy (2012)

◆ **San Bernardino City Unified School District** (San Bernardino, CA)
Hillside University Demonstration School (2016)

◆ **South Bay Union School District** (San Diego, CA)
Nestor Language Academy Charter School (2018)

◆ **Sweetwater Union High School District** (National City, CA)
Granger Junior High School (2013)
National City Middle School (2012)

Colorado

◆ **Harrison School District 2** (Colorado Springs, CO)
Centennial Elementary School (2017)
Wildflower Elementary School (2018)

Connecticut

◆ **New Haven Public Schools** (Hamden, CT)
Engineering & Science University Magnet School (2017)

Florida

◆ **Broward County Public Schools** (Ft. Lauderdale, FL)
William Dandy Middle School (2008, 2012)

◆ **Hillsborough County Public Schools** (Tampa, FL)
Muller Elementary (2006)

◆ **Miami-Dade County Public Schools** (Miami, FL)
Doral Academy Preparatory (2017)
Hialeah Gardens Middle School (2017)

Wesley Matthews Elementary (2017)

Southside Elementary Museums Magnet School (2008)

♦ **Orange County Public Schools** (Orlando, FL)

Oakshire Elementary School (2017)

♦ **School District of Palm Beach County** (West Palm Beach/Loxa-hatchee, FL)

Osceola Creek Middle School (2017)

Wynnebrook Elementary School (2017)

Georgia

♦ **Atlanta Public Schools** (Atlanta, GA):

Charles L. Gideons Elementary (2007)

West Manor Elementary (2014)

Whitefoord Elementary (2010)

♦ **Gwinnett County Public Schools** (Duluth, GA)

Harris Elementary (2015)

Illinois

♦ **Chicago Public Schools** (Chicago, Illinois)

George Washington Elementary (2014 & 2015)

♦ **Peoria Public Schools** (Peoria, Illinois)

Whittier Primary School (2006)

Kansas

♦ **Wichita Public Schools** (Wichita, KS)

Horace Mann Dual Language Magnet (2010)

Maryland

♦ **Montgomery County Public Schools** (Silver Spring, MD)

Highland Elementary School (2010)

Massachusetts

♦ **Lawrence Public Schools** (Lawrence, MA)

Community Day Charter Public School (2006)

◆ **Revere Public Schools** (Revere, MA)

Revere High School (2014)

Michigan

◆ **Detroit Edison Public Charter School** (Detroit, MI)

Detroit Edison Public School Academy (2007)

Missouri

◆ **Center School District** (Kansas City, MO)

Boone Elementary (2013)

◆ **Maplewood Richmond Heights Schools** (St. Louis/Maplewood, MO)

Maplewood Richmond Heights High School (2015)

Nevada

◆ **Clark County School District** (Las Vegas & Henderson, NV)

Fay Herron Elementary School (2018)

C.T. Sewell Elementary School (2017)

New Jersey

◆ **Newark Public Schools** (Newark, NJ)

Branch Brook School (2010)

Harriet Tubman Blue Ribbon School (2008)

New York

◆ **Mt. Vernon Public Schools** (Mt. Vernon, NY—NYC)

Cecil H. Parker Elementary School (2007)

◆ **NYC Dept. of Education** (New York City, NY)

Samuel Dupont Elementary School, P.S. 31, District #14 (2017)

Patrick Henry Preparatory School, P.S./I.S. 171, District #4 (2018)

Marble Hill High School for International Studies District #10 (2010)

◆ **Rochester City School District** (Rochester, NY)

Dr. Charles T. Lunsford School #19 (2010)

World of Inquiry Elementary (2009)

North Carolina

- **Charlotte-Mecklenburg Schools** (Charlotte, NC)
  Mallard Creek High School (2014 & 2017)
- **Durham School District** (Durham, NC)
  R.N. Harris Integrated Arts/Core Knowledge School (2012 & 2017)

Ohio

- **Cleveland Metropolitan School District** (Cleveland, OH)
  Louisa May Alcott Elementary School (2008)
  William Cullen Bryant Middle (2012)
  MC² STEM High (2012)
  Riverside School (2013)
- **Columbus Public Schools** (Columbus, OH)
  Columbus Alternative High School (2007)
- **Dayton Public Schools** (Dayton, OH)
  Dayton Business Technology High School (2013)

Oklahoma

- **Oklahoma City Public Schools** (Oklahoma City, OK)
  Linwood Elementary (2006)

Oregon

- **Self Enhancement Inc.** (Portland, OR)
  Self Enhancement Inc. Academy (2015)

Pennsylvania

- **School District of Philadelphia** (Philadelphia, PA):
  Bridesburg Elementary (2008)
  Franklin Towne Charter High School (2009)

Tennessee

- **Clarksville-Montgomery Schools** (Clarksville, TN)
  Kenwood Elementary School (2017)

♦ **Metropolitan Nashville Public Schools** (Nashville, TN)

Rose Park Math and Science Magnet (2013 & 2017)

Texas

♦ **Aldine Independent School District** (Houston, TX)

Aldine 9th Grade School (2013)

A.B. Anderson Academy (2015)

Hambrick Middle School (2010)

MacArthur Senior High School (2008 & 2013)

Ernest F. Mendel Elementary (2013)

Stehlik Intermediate (2013)

Mary Walke Stephens Elementary (2010 & 2015)

World Languages Institute (2018)

♦ **Arlington Independent School District** (Arlington, TX)

Bailey Junior High School (2017)

Juan Seguin High School (2017)

♦ **Austin Independent School District** (Austin, TX)

Dorinda L. Pillow Elementary School (2007)

♦ **Brownsville Independent School District** (Brownsville, TX)

A.X. Benavides Elementary (2015 & 2016)

Daniel Breeden Elementary (2015, 2016, 2017)

U.S. Congressman Solomon P. Ortiz Elementary (2015 & 2018)

James Pace Early College High School (2016)

Dr. Americo Paredes Elementary School (2017)

Mittie A. Pullam Elementary School (2017)

Charles Stillman Middle School (2017)

Veterans Memorial Early College High School (2016 & 2017)

Mary & Frank Yturria Elementary School (2018)

♦ **Dallas Independent School District** (Dallas, TX)

John Quincy Adams Elementary (2015)

Nathan Adams Elementary (2010)

James B. Bonham Elementary School (2009)

Jimmie Tyler Brashear Elementary (2015)

Trinidad Garza Early College High School (2012)

Walnut Hill Elementary (2015)

John J. Pershing Elementary (2015)

♦ **Fort Worth Independent School District** (Fort Worth, TX)

Bonnie Brae Elementary School (2018)

Paul Laurence Dunbar Young Men's Leadership Academy (2015 & 2018)

Marine Creek Collegiate High School (2017)

W.P. McLean Middle School (2016)

Charles A. Nash Elementary (2015)

North Hi Mount Elementary (2015)

South Hi Mount Elementary School (2016)

W.C. Stripling Middle School (2015 & 2016)

Westcliff Elementary School (2018)

♦ **Galena Park Independent School District** (Houston, TX)

Tice Elementary (2013)

♦ **Garland Independent School District** (Garland, TX)

Spring Creek Elementary School (2016)

♦ **Houston Independent School District** (Houston, TX)

Luther Burbank Elementary (2017)

Sylvan Rodriguez Elementary (2014)

George Sanchez Elementary (2014 & 2015)

E.A. "Squatty" Lyons Elementary School (2017)

♦ **Pasadena Independent School District** (Pasadena, TX)

Thompson Intermediate School (2014)

♦ **San Benito Consolidated Independent School District** (San Benito, TX)

Dr. C.M. Cash Elementary School

♦ **Sharyland Independent School District** (Mission, TX)

B.L. Gray Junior High School (2015)

♦ **Socorro Independent School District** (El Paso, TX)

Americas High School (2017)

Eastlake High School (2017)

Escontrias Elementary (2010 & 2014)

Spc. Rafael Hernando III Middle School (2016)

Mission Early College High School (2016)

♦ **Uplift Education Charter School Network** (Dallas, TX)

Uplift Education Peak Prep (2012)

♦ **Valley View Independent School District** (Pharr, TX)

Wilbur E. Lucas Elementary (2017)

♦ **Ysleta Independent School District** (El Paso, TX)

Eastwood Middle (2013 & 2014)

Virginia

♦ **Manassas City Public Schools** (Manassas, VA)

Weems Elementary (2015)

♦ **Norfolk Public Schools** (Norfolk, VA)

Dreamkeepers Academy at J.J. Roberts Elementary (2008)

♦ **Richmond Public Schools** (Richmond, VA)

Ginter Park Elementary (2006)

Thomas H. Henderson Middle School (2008)

♦ **Roanoke City Public Schools** (Roanoke, VA)

Fallon Park Elementary (2009)

Preston Park Elementary (2014)

Wasena Elementary (2015)

Washington, DC

♦ **Thurgood Marshall Academy Public Charter High School** (Washington, DC)

Thurgood Marshall Academy Public Charter High School (2014)